Reinventing Myself

Gabriele Winter

Legal Notice:

G. Euchner Consulting

c/o COCENTER

Koppoldstr. 1

86551 Aichach

Germany

Book Design by Nuno Moreira, NMDESIGN

Editor: Nicole Hall

ISBN Paperback: 978-3-9826702-0-1

ISBN E-book: 978-3-9826702-1-8

Reinventing Myself

Gabriele Winter

Inspiring stories
of a fearless woman

Introduction

In Germany, they say, a cat has seven lives. I have nine. My adventurous nature, agility, and sheer curiosity have often pushed me to my limits, sometimes even beyond them.

Ever since I was a child, my life has been a roller coaster in every area of my being, physically, emotionally, and mentally.

I was born and raised in France because my father worked all over the world as an engineer. When I was seven years old, my parents moved back to Germany, their country of origin, together with my sister and me. We got a German passport and went to a girls' school. We grew up in the mid-twentieth century and were raised to become good housewives and chefs. Lectures on cooking, sewing, and proper housekeeping were taught at our girl's school, in addition to math, physics, chemistry, geography, etc., and various languages.

My mother raised us to focus on getting married and having kids with a wealthy husband. My father was the opposite. He wanted us to go to college, get a degree, start a career, and become financially independent. He insisted on us getting good grades in school and at university. He had already earned three different academic degrees as an engineer. He wanted us to follow his lead with at least one college degree.

Both my sister and I were pushed into becoming successful by both parents, just with different visions of "success." I finished high school, went to college to study business administration, graduated with a master's degree, and pursued a successful management career in the corporate world. My sister was the creative one. She studied photography and cinema and became a successful TV director in Germany.

Despite my career in management, my bucket list of dreams was full of travel destinations and adventure. I loved and enjoyed traveling the world by myself, visiting more than sixty countries and nations over decades. I worked and lived in Iran, Switzerland, and the US. The USA has always been my favorite nation for people and lifestyle. I bought a place in Santa Fe, New Mexico, to fulfill my deeply rooted longing and dream to live in the American Southwest.

Over twenty-plus years, I spent a fortune participating in workshops about self-improvement, consciousness, and meditation, delivered by outstanding teachers and mentors like Chris Griscom, Tony Robbins, Neale D. Walsch, Deepak Chopra, Michael Beckwith, Marshall Rosenberg, and many other less famous experts. Why? I needed to dive deep into my innermost being to unveil and reconcile my family history and several traumatic experiences. With scars on my soul and memories in my heart, I wanted and needed to let go of the pain I felt when I woke up. Working with my teachers and mentors, I had to change perspectives and prejudices, dissolve inner resistances, let go, and unleash my innermost strengths, like peeling an onion to reach the core. I couldn't help but grow as a woman, changing constantly while performing a professional career and discovering my spiritual path. But still, something was missing.

One day, a friend encouraged me to remember my life's events and write them down.

"I cannot imagine what I would do if I had to face those situations you told me about. How can you remain strong and confident and still have a positive mindset? Many people would have become bitter or even depressed, but not you. When we first met, I didn't expect you to have the power, clarity, and inner strength you possess inside because you are a quiet person. It takes quite a while to get to know you, even a little bit. I was amazed by your decisiveness and get-going leadership style, which greatly impressed me. Listening to your stories of defeat, triumph, and change, I now understand where you are coming from. I want to know how you turned around situations to your favor, no matter what happened."

I started writing. With the help of Tom Schlesinger, a story architect who mentors screenwriters, novelists, and scientists on their projects from Los Angeles, I finally got the first four stories out and "on paper." Nevertheless, writing and finishing it took me ten years. Why did it take so long to write down seemingly four simple stories that had happened in my life? Because I could hardly breathe, thinking about the pain and remembering the details. I didn't want to be looking at those hurtful emotions and incidents. I tried to forget the people involved and those terrible situations. Writing finally helped release the memories from my body, mind, and soul and heal and forgive.

It was a demanding process, like a catharsis. I often got sad, angry, and cried while typing, but I also longed for the beautiful times I remembered with the people I met back then. I was amazed at the many details I saw in my inner movie.

Looking back, I am grateful for my journey, which has often forced me to change and reinvent myself—often without the help of family or friends but often with the support of strangers.

The first four stories are assembled in this book, one of the trilogy. They focus on major incidents in my private life, including significant relationships.

Book two will be about my experiences during my management career, and book three will be about discovering my spiritual path.

All the stories really happened. I want people to know what it feels like to be a woman in times of unbearable fear and crisis—unexpectedly, without any knowledge of overcoming existential challenges.

I want to encourage women to stand up again and again, no matter what happens, and bravely turn situations around in their favor. I believe everyone has a vast, unbreakable power inside. It's there—immediately and intuitively—when needed. Or, in the words of Bob Marley:

"You never know how strong you are until being strong is the only choice you have!"

That's the truth.

Courage, power, and energy are there to express. When unleashed, they will roar like lions and fight when in danger, no matter the demons of the past. You will become aware of who you are built of - each time.

Life is short. Take your chance!

Story 1: Dangerous Grounds

MUNICH, GERMANY, 2015

I had worked and lived in Zurich for more than six years, and on September 1, 2015, I moved back home to Munich, Germany. I realized that the city had changed during the past six years. It had become more crowded, and, to my surprise, I noticed many more Muslim women were wearing a black chador or burqa than I had remembered before I moved to Switzerland. On September 5, German Chancellor Angela Merkel commanded German borders to open to any refugee from war-torn Syria. Police and Border Patrol were told not to control these refugees but to let them enter, whether they had a visa for Germany or an immigration permit or a passport—or none of that at all. It was considered an act of humanity.

Why people from Syria? According to German news, the war in Syria had been unintentionally started in 2011 by some fifteen-year-old teenagers' graffiti. They had been arrested and tortured by the Syrian secret service. When their parents tried to get them out of prison, they were told, "No, you go home and make new kids." The parents were outraged, in despair, and angry. Several took to the streets to protest the regime. The Syrian government sent military and arms as a response, which made things worse.

Protests spread into other regions; some citizens obtained guns, and the civil war began. Various religious groups got involved, including ISIS, and Russia and the US stepped in. Bombs leveled entire cities to the ground. In 2015, thousands of Syrian citizens were killed, more than

15 million needed humanitarian aid, and millions escaped the country to save their lives.

The news spread over the internet that Germany would offer shelter for all Syrian refugees. However, refugees from other Middle Eastern and North African countries also made their way to Germany to take advantage of the generous aid program. They threw their passports in the trash, pretending to be Syrian at the border to receive shelter and financial support from the German social security system.

Within three months, more than two million people were estimated to have crossed the German border without being detained or registered. Sure enough, as we now know, criminals and terrorists took advantage of the open border policy and walked into Germany as well, hidden among and behind the mass of genuine refugees.

News media published pictures of the refugees arriving by train at the central station in Munich. I expected many families with little children, but what I saw shocked me. Most of the refugees depicted were young men in their twenties who seemed to be in good shape, both physically and mentally. Not one of them appeared to be traumatized or even physically hurt by the war in Syria or elsewhere. They were warmly greeted and applauded by Munich inhabitants.

I was shocked to see pictures in the media of young men covering their faces with backpacks or something else so they couldn't be identified. I knew why, and they too. They knew that video cameras were installed so the police could take pictures of them. Sure enough, they did not want to be identified and registered.

I couldn't believe that the people in Munich were so much in love with their image of being good people. Or how naive people can become after being raised in a peaceful country for seventy years. Didn't they watch the news and see what was happening worldwide? Did people seriously think that violence, murder, and rape wouldn't occur to us because we helped them, gave them money, shelter, and were supportive in every possible way?

Whenever I talked to my friends, they were astounded that I would have a different concept of young Muslim men. They didn't see the danger of a hundred thousand men coming in from totally different cultures and religions compared to our Western world, with different rules, laws, behavior patterns, and dress codes for women. The Greek saga about the fall of Troy would repeat itself in Germany.

The immigration law in Germany requires everyone to be registered within two weeks of arrival, even as a German moving within the country. That's because the government wants to keep track of people and ensure everyone pays taxes and social security fees. A few days after my return, I drove to the residents' registration office to sign up and register my new address. When I got to the building, thousands of refugees stood in line in front of it, starting from the underground train station, walking up the stairs, crossing the street, and entering the building. It was overwhelming. I looked at them in awe. It's one thing when you see a picture in the newspaper or on TV, but it's a different story when thousands of people in black clothing, chadors, and burkas stand before you.

Who were they? I had no idea how many refugees were coming in and what it would look like in person. Seeing all these people was eye-opening. I quickly identified them as Muslims because of the women's clothes: they wore their traditional chador, pants combined with long dresses and in layers, or were entirely covered in a burqa. Mostly, they were standing and walking one step behind their husbands or male relatives. This scene looked familiar to me. I glanced at their faces, and within seconds, flashbacks of my living in Tehran, Iran, almost forty years earlier fired in my head like the gunshots I had seen and heard back then. I knew immediately that this would-be act of humanity would have a terrible downside if no one took control.

It was apparent why those young men were covering their faces in front of cameras. It made me suspicious and deeply concerned. What if these young men were not looking for shelter but for a "jihad" (Holy War)? What if they were coming to attack and kill Christians and Jews for not being Muslim and not living according to the rules of the Koran—especially women? From that day on, I watched the news highly alert.

Unfortunately, the expected nightmare soon began in all major cities in Germany and other Western European countries. News appeared weekly about violent acts, rapes, and terror attacks performed by young male migrants with Islamic backgrounds. The public media discussed no other topic. Thousands of so-called refugees still arrive daily. Nobody controlled or stopped them. The nightmare had begun.

New Year's Eve has always been a special night in Germany, one spent saying goodbye to the old and welcoming the New Year with fireworks, parties, lots of dreams, hopes, and New Year's resolutions to cheer on. Despite Munich's cold, snowy winters, people go out on the street at midnight and party. We love to watch the fireworks with a glass of champagne, music playing aloud, and everybody dancing to have fun and stay warm.

My friend Sarah and I attended a theater performance on New Year's Eve 2015. Sarah has been a friend for over twenty years. She founded and successfully ran a management training company as a single mom. From the beginning, she was the first to promote my start-up company as a management consultant. We went through quite a lot together and became dear friends. I was happy to be able to catch up again with her when I came back from Zurich after so many years.

The theater we went to for the New Year's Eve performance is on a side street next to the big opera building. The Opera of Munich is right in the city's center, in a big square featuring tall columns and a wide staircase. It's a breathtaking, beautiful building. To the left is the old palace from the former kings of Bavaria, called the Residence, and across and to the right are some century-old buildings with shops and restaurants.

In between is this little theater where we made reservations for dinner and a play. The stage and chairs were in a small room in the basement. It was an independent, avant-garde–style place like those in theaters in Paris, which were famous in the twentieth. The black walls and a dimmed light barely illuminated the tables and chairs. A buffet dinner and an all-night party accompanied the theater evening. One spotlight illuminated the stage. All seats were fully taken that night because it was a funny play, thus perfect for a New Year's Eve party. Unfortunately, we had no phone connection or access to the internet down in the theater's basement. So, we enjoyed the play, food, chats, and laughter with everyone around us.

The moment the old year ends and the New Year begins is extraordinary. Minutes before, everyone gets pushed to grab a glass of champagne. It's always an exceptional moment. Nobody wants to miss it. Sarah and I grabbed a glass of champagne and went outside, excited and happy about my new and promising year in Munich. We walked toward the Opera. Unusually, it was tranquil.

"What has happened? Why is it so quiet? Where are all the people?"
I looked at Sarah.
It was weird. Nobody was on the street except for five to ten people standing at the massive staircase of the opera. We were looking at each other, wondering what was going on. Fog blocked our sight, dimming the light of

the street lamps. Nobody said a word or talked to each other while we walked closer. It was so quiet that I could hear my breathing. It felt like standing in a cemetery. I got scared, expecting someone to scream at any moment.

When we arrived at the opera, we walked up the stairs to better view the rest of the square and watch the fireworks. Usually, hundreds of people gather at the place to party, even fifteen minutes before midnight, when most people start with their fireworks.

No one made any attempts; nothing was to be seen or heard. It was spooky.

Suddenly, Sarah's mobile phone started to ring, and the ringing sound of text messages coming in didn't seem to stop. Wi-Fi worked outside the theater.

"We have a terror alarm at two train stations in Munich, one at the main station nearby and the other at a big train hub outside Munich."

"What? What???" I stared at Sarah in disbelief.

"Yes. Look. Several messages from friends and family advise us not to take a train at the main train station to get home."

"What happened?"

We were frozen with fear when we heard the dark, calm sound of the grand midnight bell ringing from the famous Theatine church.

"Our little theater is the safest place around here. We should not stand outside when a terrorist attack is expected to break out nearby at any moment."

"What shall we do?" Sarah looked at me.

"I don't know yet. But the theater is the safest place right now. And by the way, cheers to a healthy and happy New Year 2016."

I raised my glass to her and a few others standing beside us. I couldn't help but make it sound ironic. Sarah didn't understand where I came from and why I reacted harshly. I had never told my story of when I was trapped in the first-ever jihad in Iran in 1978.

Nobody said a word. We were speechless, literally frozen. Our fired-up party mood was gone in a second. Somebody shot a few fireworks in the sky.

Back at the theater, one man had received the news, too. He gave us more details on the planned terror attack, which still could happen. It was not over yet.

"Somebody announced that secret services from several countries discovered various terrorist attacks to be placed in the US and Europe, organized by the Islamic State of Iraq and the Levant (ISIL), targeting New Year's celebration night. Several major European cities, including Paris, London, and Moscow, have unprecedented security measures. Also, Munich is under attack."

He continued, "In Munich, ISIL terrorists reportedly had planned attacks on two train stations on New Year's Eve. The main station and the other one outside of Munich serve the smaller cities in the countryside."

"We can try to get a taxi," Sarah suggested, knowing that it had always been impossible to get a taxi on a typical New Year's Eve party night, let alone with the threat of two potential terrorist attacks.

"That's too scary," I replied. Why don't we book a room for one night in one of the nearby hotels? We would be safe, continue to party, sleep well, and safely go home tomorrow morning after a nice breakfast." I loved the idea and tried to convince her.

"Do you know how expensive that would be? Five hundred dollars per night would be the minimum. I don't want to pay that huge amount for a night in a hotel in my hometown. That's weird. I will walk toward the train station, and if I don't find a taxi, I will take the risk and take a train," she said while shaking her head.

"But what if the trains are not running at all? What if every street around the train station is blocked, and you can't even pass it using a taxi?" I was catching my breath.

"I would only stay in a hotel in the worst case. But you can go and find a hotel. That's okay with me, don't worry."

"Are you kidding me? No way. It's a long walk. I'd be worried knowing you're marching to the train station alone at night. That's not safe at all. If something happens to you, I will regret it for the rest of my life. I will come with you."

I gave up. Sarah seemed careless. She had no sense of what could happen. She was innocent because she had never seen a bomb explode nearby, except on a TV screen. But I experienced it firsthand in Tehran, Iran. I had noticed the bombs exploding, and I had heard from my bedroom when a man shot a woman in a verbal fight late in the evening— the killer must have been either her husband or a relative. The silence after the gunshot was horrible. I had been afraid to step out. He would have killed me for witnessing it. I remember the sound of the bombs and that murder every time I hear fireworks or see lightning strikes.

It was the first time Islamists violently turned a democratically governed country into an Islamic state.

All my memories came back that night in Munich. I was afraid, but I didn't tell Sarah anything about what I had experienced in Iran. I did not want her to get scared or panicked. We grabbed our winter coats, exchanged high heels for winter boots, put on gloves, and said goodbye to the other guests. They continued partying. When we stepped outside, the air was icy. The freezing, humid fog made it feel even worse, and we could see our breath like little plumes of steam coming out of our noses and mouths. The fog dimmed all the colorful Christmas lights on the street and decorations on the buildings. It was quiet. No sound. Nobody was on the road anymore.

I learned from my father, a former elite paratrooper in World War II, that when in danger, I must become invisible, physically and emotionally, using my senses. In other words, freeze, don't make exaggerated moves, and don't look up and around but down. If you meet someone, don't look into their eyes. Prevent eye contact under any circumstances because it could reveal your fear. Don't speak a word; breathe shallowly. Walk on your toes so nobody can hear you. Get yourself mentally and emotionally ice-cold. Stop thinking any thoughts or recalling any emotional patterns.

I grabbed Sarah's arm and walked toward the central train station, a twenty- to thirty-minute walk on a snowy, icy street at minimum. I watched Sarah silently. Interestingly enough, she copied my body language instinctively. We quietly disappeared in the fog. Only our boots made creaky sounds while walking on the snow.

No one is around us. That is not a good sign, I thought. I was scared to death. My heart beat loudly and heavily against my chest. I could hardly breathe.

Neither one of us said a word.

We passed several hotels where people came out, leaving their New Year's Eve parties. They were looking for taxi cabs. We also wanted to catch one of them, but there was no chance. Men in their tuxedos were running faster than we were to get them. We continued walking, heads down. When we got closer to the central train station, we saw many people on the street, looking for a train or tram. They, too, were trying to find a way to get home. All roads around the station were blocked for cars by police barricades. At the center of one central hub for trams, we stopped and checked when the following trams would leave for my home. We waited more than an hour for the next one to arrive. It started snowing again. We were freezing despite our winter coats and boots.

At 3:00 a.m., a train finally arrived. It was fully packed with people, and we had difficulty squeezing ourselves into it. No one wanted to be left alone near the central train station where the terrorist attack was supposed to happen. We made our way to one of the windows because I wanted to see what was happening outside. Everyone was silent, although New Year's Eve was the party night. I looked around. Some people wore precious evening gowns and jewelry. I saw the fear in their eyes, wondering whether they would arrive safely or be robbed on their way home. Some were standing right in the middle of the train, eyes closed. It looked like they were silently praying. The second stop was supposed to be at the main central train station, allegedly the next location for the attack. The train didn't stop but slowly continued moving toward, then past it. We all held our breath, waiting for a bomb to explode any second.

"I don't understand why the train driver goes so slow because it would give a terrorist enough time to target our train, and then *wham*," I said.

Sarah shrugged.

"Maybe he has been told to do so."

"I can't believe that. Terrorist experts should know and tell a driver what to do and how to do it. Even the bus drivers in Egypt know that. When sitting in a bus traveling to an ancient tourist spot, they drive very fast through every village in the desert so they don't get stopped by a terrorist, kidnapper, or robber."

I shook my head and kept looking out the window.

Suddenly, I saw a special operation force of at least twenty SWATs at the train station. They were heavily dressed and armed to their teeth with machine guns, bulletproof jackets, and helmets. The entity of the train station building was shut off and dark. We could barely see into it. Nobody seemed to be in there except these courageous SWAT heroes walking around. They had everything and everyone under control. I felt safe for the first time. I was grateful and knew these guys would protect us, no matter what.

"Did you see them?" I turned to Sarah.

"Yes, these SWATs look pretty scary," she replied.

"No, not to me. I am glad they are here, and these guys protect us, even risking their lives for us."

Sarah didn't understand what I was trying to tell her and didn't recognize our danger. The train passed the station and continued. I was relieved. Finally, we got home safely. It was over. I offered Sarah overnight accommodation at my guest's place, allowing her to continue her way home the following day safely. She nodded. I opened a bottle of champagne at home, and we cheered again for a happy ending and a safe New Year 2016. It was 5:30 a.m. when I finally fell asleep.

We heard it on the news. The police in Munich stated that they had thwarted the terrorist plots after they received a concrete tip that an attack was expected at 7:40 p.m. on New Year's Eve. Secret services in the United States and France gave a hint. German police shut off the train stations immediately. They cleared all streets and nearby areas from pedestrians. According to the Bavarian government, not only two but up to seven suicide bombers had planned to blow themselves up at different locations in Munich, including the two train stations. We were lucky to have survived.

That night, all my memories of the revolution in Iran woke up again. I remembered the terror, scenes of violence, the overwhelming fear of death when controlled by the military, and not being able to escape for several weeks. I remembered all of it and many more outrages that have occurred since.

MOSCOW, SOVIET UNION, 1978

After finishing my bachelor's degree in business administration and before continuing to earn my master's degree, I decided to get some international experience. I applied for a work scholarship at the International Association of Students in Economics and Business (AIESEC) in a foreign country. AIESEC is a well-known global organization that helps students work as interns in companies worldwide. I wanted to boost my future career by having international work experience. I got approved and received three offers from companies in Africa and the Middle East. One job opportunity was offered in Lagos, Nigeria, the other in Accra, Ghana, and the third company I could work at was in Tehran, Iran.

I decided to go to gorgeous, booming Tehran in my early twenties. It had four million people and is nestled next to the Alborz Mountains, which separate the city from the lavish Caspian Sea. Iran is bordered by Turkmenistan in the north, the Persian Gulf in the south, Iraq to the west, and Afghanistan and Pakistan to the east. A friend advised me not to go for a weekend trip to Afghanistan, a country already in trouble politically and economically back then, even though it was seemingly open to Western lifestyle and culture, but, in reality, it was punished by terrorists and rebels. I had no urge to put my toe into the water and test the temperature.

Iran, also known as Persia, was considered the center of emerging business and financial growth and was on its way to democracy, adapting to the prosperity of Western countries. The Shah-in-Shah (the emperor) Reza Pahlavi led the nation. Persia has a history of over three thousand years of brilliant minds, literature, art, culture, architecture, design, and science, which you can still recognize in their people. I remember that Iranians didn't walk but paced with a straight body, proud head, and chin up. You can sense their ancient history in their body language and genes.

Iranians are extraordinary people whom I have always admired for their richness of ancient culture and history. In the seventies, women wore makeup and the latest fashion of the Western world. They didn't cover themselves up with a chador or a full burqa, except when entering a mosque. In some countries, there is a similar rule for women in a Christian, Jewish, or Orthodox church. Wearing a scarf had been banned by the father of the Shah in the 1940s. Back then, the people of Persia practiced three religions: Islam, Christianity, and Judaism. The Shah and his family, like most Persians, were Muslims. However, they were also the most progressive supporters of Western lifestyles. They opened the country's borders to the world, letting foreign people create businesses and fostering growth and prosperity for the nation. Bringing in foreign companies and creating new jobs was perceived as the most significant opportunity to lead the country into wealth and development.

I was happy to get a job as a marketing assistant in a market research institute—co-owned by Iranian and American partners. The team was small, with ten employees in total. At that time, the American partner had lived in Tehran for twelve years, so he knew the country and its people quite well, that is, as best as they would allow him to enter their world.

After signing the final AIESEC papers and booking my flight to Tehran, I sat in the plane with a stopover in Moscow on the morning of July 14th, 1978. The trip included a sightseeing tour of Moscow before connecting to Tehran.

Going on such a trip back then was a real adventure for everyone because Germany was still divided by the wall, a deathtrap separating Germany into two parts: West Germany (capitalistic) and East Germany (communistic). The wall that ran through the two German states and Berlin separated Germany and all communist-led states in Eastern Europe from the Western world. Back then, the Soviet Union was a conglomerate of several communist states led by dictators. Moscow was the capital of the Soviet Union and the headquarters for those Eastern European communist states. The wall had been the symbolic "Iron Curtain," which cut off all people from Poland, Hungary, today's Czech Republic, Bulgaria, Ukraine, and others. People living in communist countries were not allowed to travel to the Western parts of the world. Each time someone from East Germany tried to escape or even visit one of the Western countries, they were either arrested or shot right at the wall.

Nonetheless, I was excited to take the trip to Moscow and then work in Tehran.

"I am doing it!" I told my friends. I wanted to see Moscow, the beautiful Kremlin, the buildings, the churches, and how people live there.

During my flight to Moscow, I sat beside a friendly and likable German couple. They also were on a trip to Iran. Michael and Karen were high school teachers in their mid-thirties, married. Michael was quite tall: black jeans, black shirt, hair, beard, and black-rimmed glasses. With her long dark hair, Karen dressed colorfully, like a typical Hippie-girl in the seventies. I liked them the minute I saw them. They wanted to visit their German friends in Tehran and were also looking forward to traveling to the countryside of Iran. They said the country and the cities are beautiful. They wanted to see the desert in the south and the tropical vegetation in the Caspian Sea in the north. I was fascinated when listening to their descriptions and got excited to start my new adventure in Tehran.

The agency told me I would arrive in Moscow around noon and land in Tehran in the late evening of the same day. I organized for someone from AIESEC to pick me up at the airport in Tehran and bring me to the hostel for female students. The day after my arrival was scheduled as my first day at work in the market research company.

My father, who had worked as an engineer and expat in Novosibirsk, Siberia, advised me on how to behave in Russia. He insisted on respecting and understanding that everyone in Eastern Europe or the Soviet Union was at the mercy of the police, military, and administration, regardless of nationality.

"No discussion, no nagging questions, or even complaints are allowed. It's perceived as disrespectful. Either you do what they say, or you get arrested, or worse. Opposition or provocatively playing against their rules will be heavily punished. Do not dare or try to stretch your limits."

I wasn't thinking about his advice, but when we landed in Moscow, I was slightly worried about the stopover. It was a different story dealing with police in West Germany compared to police in a country led by the military, who controlled people 24/7 and directly showed off their power.

We felt this control clearly when we arrived at the Moscow airport, although we were set as transit passengers. We were standing in line at passport control; it was my turn. The German couple was waiting right behind me. The Russian immigration officer looked at me, looked at my passport and flight ticket, took them away, and commanded me to step aside with a hand gesture and some words in Russian. I was confused and frightened immediately.

I turned around and looked at the German couple for help, hoping they would say something or ask the officer what was happening.

"What shall I do?"

But they shrugged and shook their heads. They had no idea, either. The Russian officer repeated his words harshly at me and made it clear to step aside.

Then, he checked the passports and flight tickets of the German couple. He looked at them, also took their passports and flight tickets, and commanded the same: step aside and wait.

Finally, all transit passengers with a connecting flight to Tehran or any other city had to go aside. We were twelve people, separated from the other passengers. Anxiously, we looked into each other's eyes, wondering what would happen next.

An armed border patrol agent arrived and ordered us to follow them. Our little group walked behind them like prisoners, and that's how I felt. Everyone looked at us. We followed the border police through the hall and downstairs to a separate room in the basement of the building: walls, stairs—all made of gray concrete. The border patrol agent requested us to wait in the windowless room with fluorescent lights and some uncomfortable chairs, sentineled by a soldier armed to his teeth.

Now, I was terrified. I remembered the stories my father told me from working in Siberia. Because border patrol took away our passports and flight tickets, it became apparent that we were no longer human beings in the eyes of the Russian government. Destroying our flight tickets and passports would mean deleting our registration, thus our identity and existence. It would make our traces stop at the Moscow airport, and then we would have disappeared. No one would ever find us if they killed and buried us somewhere in the vast Russian wilderness.

My mind was swirling. What if they took us to one of those dreaded labor camps in Siberia or Mongolia called gulags?

"This feels like we're being arrested!" I shouted, looking at the soldier and then at Michael and Karen.

"This is the first time that they've treated us like this. This didn't happen the first time we traveled to Tehran via Moscow," Karen replied.

"We haven't done anything wrong." I looked at her.

"How can they dare to take us hostage for nothing? Are we arrested now? What do we do?"

I had a layover before connecting to Tehran. I could still make it. I tried to calm myself down. I would need to skip the sightseeing tour in Moscow, which would be more than okay. I was desperate, sensing I would miss my connecting flight to Tehran. The people from AIESEC would be waiting for me at the airport in the middle of the night. What would they do when they realized I wouldn't be on board the connecting flight?

Suddenly, I couldn't wait to leave Russia. I was not too fond of a country that treated tourists and guests like criminals. A mixture of fear and anger climbed up my throat. I looked at the soldier, but he didn't show any reaction.

"He doesn't understand you," said another passenger.

"He only speaks Russian. But even if he could speak English, he wouldn't answer. Better to say nothing and wait."

We looked at one another with fearful eyes. The media in Germany had covered horrible stories about border patrols in East Germany and Russia. We knew what could happen—but did we know the full extent?

Another passenger, who spoke Russian, looked at the guard.

"What will happen next?" he said in Russian.

He did not get an answer.

"We have connecting flights; we will miss them if you don't let us go!"
He tried again. No answer. There was no glimpse in the eyes or a mimic in the face of the border police.

"Will they let us call the travel agency, parents, or the German embassy?"

"Nope, not possible. They won't let everyone call their respective embassy. It takes too much time and effort," one of the passengers replied.

Back then, we had no chance to speak with the border patrol, ask questions, leave the room, or call home or the embassy. We were detained against our will, which was illegal. We couldn't do anything about it; we were trapped.

I gave up. I stopped thinking and surrendered. I accepted the situation and let go of my fear. My anxiety disappeared slowly. It took a while, and then those feelings were gone. Emotional coldness took over internally.

What the heck! I felt empty and exhausted. I gave up. I sat down, staring into space. Michael put his hand on my shoulder.

"We'll be good. Don't worry."

I looked up at him and shrugged. I couldn't feel anything.

I recalled my father's warnings, urging me to obey whatever the Russians would command me to do.

He told me not to make any comments or take pictures while on my sightseeing tour. How much more true were his words in my current situation!

"Always be low-key and do what they say," he advised. "If something happens and you get caught, they will punish you and probably imprison you. So be careful and do exactly what the Russians command," he told me. He was worried but knew he couldn't stop me from taking the trip and doing what I wanted. I was his adventure-seeking, courageous daughter, a mirror of his personality, and he understood.

We couldn't predict what would happen next and couldn't do anything about it. We felt helpless and without control, and we felt horrible. As a student, I was used to always looking for solutions. This time, though, striving to escape the situation would have been the wrong approach.

Nobody said a word. Everyone was in shock, and we held our breath.

After seemingly endless hours of waiting without water or a restroom, the door opened. Two border control officers came in and said something in Russian. The one guy among us who spoke Russian started translating.

"They want us to follow them to the room where our luggage is stored."

A glimpse of hope returned. Everyone was grateful that they had taken care of our suitcases. We looked at each other with relief and followed them with heads down as if they were leading us to the scaffold. My heart was racing in my throat. They directed us to the storage room. After everything, a hopefully cheerful ending appeared one where they would lead us to our connecting flights.

That was a false assumption. We picked up our suitcases and continued to follow the officers. Still, no one spoke a word. We wandered endless corridors of gray, fluorescently lit labyrinths until we approached a narrow staircase. To our surprise, the border patrol commanded us to follow the stairs outside the building and board the bus waiting there. Leaving the building and breathing fresh air was a relief, although it was hot and humid outside. It was already dark. We needed clarification. A bus? They did not lead us back to the airport.

"Where will they take us? What they're doing is illegal. I want to speak with the German Embassy," one guy said forcefully into the group. "Can you tell the border patrol that we want to speak with the German Embassy, please?" he asked, looking at the guy who spoke Russian.

"There is nobody to talk to," he replied. "The border patrol and bus driver won't help us. They have different commands. Let's wait and see where they will take us."

He seemed very calm. Maybe he was our protecting angel. We followed as he recommended.

What would happen to my connecting flight to Tehran? What would the AIESEC people do, waiting for me at the airport? The connecting flight would take off without the German couple and me. That was for sure.

No questions were allowed. I felt sorry for myself and almost cried. I had made the wrong decision.

"Whoever will run into mischief will be killed." Suddenly, that saying somehow

occurred in my mind, and I couldn't stop repeating the thought.

My adventurous, exciting trip started poorly, although I was relieved to leave the dungeon. How little did I know about the world, politics, and humans outside my comfortable, democratic, peaceful home and Western culture in Germany? Next to nothing. I had to learn my lesson.

It was too late and useless to regret making the wrong decision. I had been too naïve and didn't research enough to imagine what could happen. Instead of booking a non-stop flight to Tehran, I wanted to save money and bought a cheaper flight with a stopover in Moscow. Big mistake, but there was no turning back now. After all, without a passport and a ticket, there was nothing else to do but sit humbly on the bus, waiting for whatever would come or whoever would show up and tell us what to do next.

We got onto the bus, and then it took off. We had no idea where the Russians would bring us. And we were not allowed to talk to each other, either.

The bus started its engine. An endless number of gray high-rise apartment blocks passed by. *That must be the city of Moscow. Why would a government have its people live like that - in huge barrack-like buildings without any chance to get out into the world, enjoy life and cultural diversity, and discover nature's beauty?*

Back then, Moscow was a dark city with few street lights—no monuments, restaurants, or illuminated shops as we know it today. Poverty was everywhere, clearly visible. Russian cars released dark, air-polluting smoke in front and behind our bus. Only a few people were on the street, their clothes gray and black, the same color as the buildings. It seemed everyone and everything was hiding in this soup of gray-and-black, mysterious something.

The bus stopped in front of a shabby hostel next to downtown Moscow's central train station.

"Get out, take your luggage, and walk into the lobby!" the bus driver commanded in Russian.

We got off the bus and had to enter the hostel lobby with our suitcases. There was a wooden reception table, a small lamp on the desk, and a chair behind it, all in front of a gray wall. Across was a tall window facing the street, and next to it was the entrance. That was it. White fluorescent lights on the ceiling and shiny linoleum floor were the style of this straightforward Russian hostel in the 70s. Behind the desk, a full-figured Russian woman was waiting in her dark gray uniform. Her hair was combed into a bun. Her expression gave her the appearance of a stern soldier. She asked for our names and handed a room key to each of us. We were commanded to go into our rooms and stay there. Everyone nodded.

I went to my room. It was small, merely bigger than the size of the single bed, but clean, at least. I put my suitcase aside, went to the bathroom, washed my hands, and went back downstairs to the receptionist. I was thirsty and hungry.

I had a small number of US dollars in my pocket because no one could bring Rubles, the Russian currency, into the country. I asked the receptionist if I could buy some snacks, but she refused. I was looking for a vending machine providing snacks or water, but there wasn't any. I asked to go to the train station nearby to buy some snacks. She refused.

The train station was around the corner, an easy walk away. I knew my US dollars would be highly welcomed, as US currency was the most valued currency in Russia. When the receptionist saw me walking toward the exit, she rushed over to the door, stopped, stood with her feet wide apart and her hands on her hips, and blocked it.

"Njet, Njet," she said, shaking her head. She looked at me, quite upset. I tried to explain with my hands that I was hungry and thirsty and wanted to buy something to eat and return. She shook her head. I showed her my dollar notes. She did not let me pass. I had no chance. She was stronger than me. I gave up. I tried to think positively: *It's for a reason.*

So, I was to have no food or drink for the night, not even a glass of water. I didn't want to drink the tap water from the bathroom, which stank of chemicals. I was tired. I locked my room and sat on my bed, feeling lost, alone, abandoned, and profoundly helpless for the first time.

"What have I done?"

"Anyone who puts themselves in danger will die from it," I remembered the words of my grandma.

I had no passport or ticket, and nobody knew what I was going through or where I was.

I tried to calm down - told myself to be patient and surrender everything to God. I had to trust and stop thinking about what could happen next and in the upcoming days. I couldn't think any further out in time. In my experience, surrendering to my situation and accepting what had happened kept me from getting too emotionally involved and thus utterly freaking out, which would have made things worse.

Without a passport or a ticket and not enough money, I would not be able to continue my trip. I would not even be able to go back home to Germany. During the era of the Iron Curtain, Russians would not let me or the others cross the border into another country. I was trapped. Would I have to live in Russia for the rest of my life? How could I make a living?

What would happen to the group? Would we be shipped somewhere and sold by human traffickers? Or would we be considered suitable for a deal between Russia and Germany, exchanged as hostages as often seen in the news those days? Anything was possible.

Every reason for being detained seemed realistic. On the one hand, we were not that important to anyone, but who knew what strategic ideas these political chess players had in mind? I should have faith that the nightmare would soon come to an end. Exhausted, hungry, thirsty, and fully dressed, I fell in a dreamless sleep on my bed.

I woke up in the middle of the night to someone hammering on my door, yelling something in Russian. I was shocked and frightened to death. I had yet to realize where I was. After a few seconds, it dawned on me. I looked at my watch—three o'clock in the morning. Someone hammered at my door again and repeated what he was yelling before.

I decided to get up, and on my toes, I walked to the door. I didn't want to open the door or make any noise, pretending I was not there. I put my ear to the door, listening to the noise outside. I held my breath, and my heart was pounding. What if he was a human trafficker? I waited.

Then, I heard his steps disappearing. It became quiet again. There was no sound anymore. Stillness.

Get out of here, get out of this prison!
My inner voice was yelling at me immediately.

I didn't even brush my teeth. I grabbed my bags and rushed down the stairs to the reception. I was still in my clothes from the day before. The other transit passengers were already at the reception, tired and looking just as confused as I was.

"Does anyone know what's going on and what will happen next?"

The German businessman who could speak Russian asked the receptionist. She shook her head and shrugged. We realized our trip would finally continue and hoped they would return us to the airport. I went straight to the German couple, Michael and Karen, and asked them what was happening. They did not know either. So, together, we waited for further instructions.

The old, shabby bus from the previous night stood in front of the hotel. The receptionist unlocked the hotel door, and the Russian driver harshly told us to board the bus before putting our suitcases into the trunk. He treated us disrespectfully, almost like criminals, though none of us had done anything harmful to anyone. We were innocent transit passengers, each on individual paths to other countries.

It was quiet in the middle of the night when we took off driving through the city. It was darker than the evening before when we arrived. Streetlights were turned off, and the lights of some cars or trucks driving toward us lit the street for mere seconds.

When we left Moscow, it got even darker—we could see nothing except the front light of our shabby bus, which was shaking and shuddering because of the lousy street conditions.

Nobody spoke a word. Everyone closed their eyes and merely went back to sleep. Regardless of the silence, everyone could feel the tension and anxiety underneath, not knowing where they would bring us or what was about to happen.

After a one-hour drive, we saw the lights of the Moscow airport approaching. A sigh of relief was heard throughout the bus. We would get out of here.

The airport hall was already bursting with people and noise. It was utter chaos, and yelling was the only way to communicate with anyone. Everyone seemed to be afraid of not being able to escape, to get out of hell. We grabbed our bags and had to wait at the entrance door. Again, two security men armed to the teeth accompanied us to the check-in counter. I said my name, checked in my bag, and finally got my boarding pass to Tehran.

"And my passport and ticket?" I asked.

The check-in steward shook his head. No passports or tickets were handed out.
I asked again, but he pretended not to understand me.

I waited until the German couple got their boarding passes. We walked through passport control and security checks by showing our boarding passes. They knew who we were and just waved us through it. All of us whose connecting flights were to Tehran approached the requested gate. Then, another bus picked us up because all airplanes were usually parked outside on the airfield.

With only a few of us heading toward Tehran, the bus driver brought us to an empty plane with open doors. We were the first passengers to board. Everyone looked for their seat, sat down, and kept waiting. One after another, more and more passengers boarded the plane. After boarding was completed, the Russian border patrol came into the airplane. We looked at each other, again frightened and holding our breath. We were already traumatized.

"Will they pick us up and take us to some unknown place like last night?" My hands were shaking. Tears of fear welled in my eyes.

They called us transit passengers one by one by name, approached each one, and gave back our passports and tickets. Then they left the plane.
The nightmare was over.

The plane took off. After it finally reached its cruising altitude, the stewardess announced the flight to Tehran. Michael, Karen, and I looked at each other, shaking our heads in disbelief. Tears of relief were rolling down my face.

I took a deep breath. I felt like I had aged by ten years during the last twenty-four hours.

"What was that?"
We looked at each other. Everyone had the same thoughts. How could that have happened?

"I told you, all will be good," Michael said joyfully. He had been frightened and was relieved as well.

"I need a drink. I am sure Karen does, too," he continued. She nodded her head.

"Me too. But I need a bottle of water first. I am thirsty. We had no water for at least eighteen hours," I replied.

We ordered water and vodka and celebrated our newfound freedom.

We were grateful and felt blessed. For the first time in my life, I discovered and appreciated the vast value of personal freedom and what it really means: it is the essential value and right of every human being, next to perfect health.

And it's not for free or to be taken for granted.

I regained control over my life again. For the first time, I realized how critical freedom and freedom of choice is. Since then, it has become the most valuable right in my life, guiding me in every sense, every situation or relationship.

During our flight, we discussed why the Russians had detained us. Nobody had an explanation or clue. It was illegal, that was for sure. Human rights? Forget about that in a communist-led dictatorship back then. The blocking Iron Curtain was the shield that made it possible.

Back then, arbitrary detainment was possible due to the lack of public transparency, no internet, no mobile phones or social media, and lack of TV coverage or news. People were easily threatened, controlled, and steered. If we had rebelled and protested, they would have punished us in a far worse way or even killed and buried us in the middle of nowhere—and nobody in the world would have taken notice.

Would any of us or our families file lawsuits against Russia for unlawfully detaining us? No. Not at all. No chance.

Nobody from our home government would have listened in the long run or would have even cared because we were not significant enough to anyone except our families.

I was grateful to have escaped Moscow and finally been on my way to Tehran.

TEHRAN, IRAN, 1978

After a three-hour flight during which we watched the landscape change from mountains and green fields into the deserts of sand, we landed safely. We entered immigration anxious, wondering if the awful experience in Moscow would repeat itself. Would they hold us back and detain us, too? To my surprise, the police at the passport control were friendly.

Thank God, passports and customs were very easy to pass. What I didn't know at that time was that I had signed a blank check for my life in Iran. I walked to the baggage claim, grabbed my luggage from the belt, and looked around for Michael and Karen. They were looking for me, too, to say goodbye.

"What's next?" Michael asked me.

"I hope the AIESEC people are here to pick me up."

"I am sure they have realized what happened and will pick you up. Well then, have a wonderful time. Enjoy your new job, and get to see Tehran and the countryside of Iran as well. "

"It will be beautiful," Karen added.

"Here is the phone number of our German friends where we will stay for the first two weeks of our trip. Just in case you need help. In difficult situations, it's easier to speak with someone from your home country who speaks your language," Michael looked at me.

"Thank you. It's appreciated. I am very grateful." I anxiously replied. I feared being left alone now and had no idea what to expect next.

"Bob works as an engineer for a major German corporation in Tehran. His wife Ellen takes care of their two little sons." Karen added.

"Thank you so much."

I hugged them and walked to the arrival hall. A massive crowd of hundreds of men stood at the gate in a half circle. They were suntanned, with wrinkled faces, black hair, and black beards, and dressed in kaftans. No women were among them, which caught me off-guard. I didn't expect to see only men.

They gazed at me in surprise, too, with wide-open eyes, checking on me from head to toe and seemingly undressing me. I realized they rarely saw a white woman with blonde hair and blue eyes dressed in jeans and a sweater walking alone.

I looked around, searching for the AIESEC staff who were to pick me up. I pushed myself through the crowd of men from one end of the airport hall to the other, looking for a sign with my name. Nobody was there. No, nothing at all.

Standing amid the male crowd, I was stumped. Men approached and yelled at me, grabbing my luggage, arms, and shoulders and offering a taxi ride or baggage transportation.

For the second time in twenty-four hours, I deeply regretted my adventurous spirit and curiosity to discover the world, thinking that no one and nothing would harm me. I had made a big mistake, expecting a trip to Tehran to be as easy as flying to London. I considered going to the airline at the departure level and rescheduling my flight home to Germany. I also needed more cash to stay in a hotel for one night. And I didn't want to spend a night at the airport alone, sitting on a bench, watching my bag among these men.

My life was on a silk thread again.

"Is anybody coming to pick you up?"

I turned around. Karen and Michael appeared right behind me while looking for their friends.

"AIESEC must have forgotten me because of the delay of our flight. I can't believe how careless they are. I don't know what to do now. I might fly back to Germany tomorrow if I can change my ticket."

I was exhausted, disappointed, and sad that my adventure to Iran would end like this.

"But that would be a pity. We will ask our German friends here if you can stay with them and us for at least one night, and AIESEC can pick you up tomorrow," Michael replied.

"Tomorrow, you could safely call AIESEC, and then you will know your next step!" Karen encouraged me.

"Thank you so much. I deeply appreciate your support. Let's do that."

I thanked God for bringing such caring, loving people into my life. I was profoundly grateful and relieved to have met these strangers and received a night of safety—free of charge. The three of us made our way to the exit, where Ed and Ellen were waiting.

Bob, my new host, resembled a surfer from Southern California: tall, slim body, suntanned skin, blonde hair, a big mustache, and a big grin. He seemed to be in his early forties. Ellen herself was tall, too, thin, with long, blonde hair, blue eyes, and a big, welcoming smile.

They both joyfully greeted Michael and Karen.

"How are you? How was your flight? We expected you a day earlier. What happened?" Bob asked.

"We will tell you what happened later at your home. I want to introduce you to Gabby."

They all looked at me.

"The organization that was supposed to pick her up didn't show up. Nobody is here," I tried to explain.

Michael quickly explained who I was and the purpose of my trip to Tehran.

"Is there an opportunity for her to stay at your house for just one night? She has no other place to go."

"Sure, no problem. We have enough room for everyone." Ellen smiled at me, nodding her head, and grabbed my bag.

I was deeply grateful for their offer. I must have had angels at my side all along my trip. Indeed, these strangers would become my protecting angels and even friends for the following months, which I didn't realize then. The three of us squeezed into the back seat of their Range Rover, and we happily drove through the illuminated night in Tehran to their home in the northern part of the city, close to the Shah Palace. I looked out the window, watching the people walking along the street, the signs of little shops, stores, open-door kitchens, restaurants, and street names, all in Persian letters. I couldn't read anything at all. I was in awe of discovering an entirely new world and culture in every sense, and I was far away from my home in Germany, which was so different.

Bob, an engineer who worked for a big German corporation, and Ellen, his wife, and two sons, had no interest in returning to Germany. They were happy where they were. Apart from the adventure of living abroad, being an expat family is quite challenging, but it includes a much more comfortable lifestyle than living in Germany. I know this because my father was an expat engineer for his entire life. My mom, sister, and I accompanied him many times. Living as an expat in foreign countries means being respected and appreciated by many, but not everyone. You are perceived as a guest and, indeed, must obey the country's laws, follow the rules of the hosts and employers, investigate and adapt to cultural differences, and learn the language. Without knowledge of the language, speaking, and reading, any integration into society will fail.

Tehran is a huge metropolitan city. A vast desert divided the northern part of the city from the southern part back then, thus separating the rich people living in the north with a cool breeze compared to the poor in the south. Bob and Ellen's house was high up in the north of Tehran, near the Niavaran Palace of the Shah family and close to the Elburz Mountains. The energy was much more relaxed and calm, and the air was less polluted compared to the south. Parks, trees, water channels along the streets, and lavish gardens full of blooming flowers marked this wealthy residential area of Persian families and expats.

Bob and Ellen's house was a perfect four-bedroom place with a garden and a swimming pool surrounded by a fence of tall green bushes. Nobody could look inside. My lifestyle as a student in Germany had been quite different—a small apartment without a garden or a patio. I was impressed and loved this house from the first moment I saw it. Who wouldn't?

That evening, we sat outside by the pool, drinking wine as Michael, Karen, and I told my new friends about our incredible story of our Moscow detainment. We were celebrating life again, like a second birthday party.

Late at night, I went into my bedroom, exhausted. I crashed into a deep sleep in a safe environment. After swimming in the pool, coffee, and breakfast the following day, I felt I had arrived in paradise. What a gift I had received from the universe.

At last, I called AIESEC. The girl on the phone had no idea who I was. They were surprised and had not expected my arrival. Either AIESEC in Germany had missed telling them, or they had completely forgotten to pick me up at the airport. Their excuse was that they thought I had changed my mind without letting them know. That was a poor apology. Thinking about what I had gone through the previous forty-eight hours, having been all alone at the airport in Tehran in the middle of the night, I got upset about their attitude. I considered it as irresponsible and reckless.

The same afternoon, some students from AIESEC arrived to pick me up. I said goodbye to Bob, Ellen, Michael, and Karen.

"Call us if you don't like where you will stay," Bob insisted. "You can stay with us as long as you want."

"Awww, thank you so much. I appreciate your offer. Thank you so much to each of you for what you have done for me. I am and will be deeply grateful for the rest of my life. I will call you and keep you posted about what's going on here. Maybe we can meet for dinner one night."

I smiled, hugged everyone, and left my new friends saddened. I already missed them. But I was relieved to have a plan B for returning to them if things didn't work out—just in case. As I had so recently learned, you never know. I lost a lot of trust and confidence in organizations like AIESEC when they were not at the airport to pick me up. I had not expected such careless behavior from this worldwide organization. I learned my lesson. Being in a foreign country with a different culture, religion, and social rules for women, especially, I realize now I was lucky to have found new friends I could rely on to help in an emergency.

*   *   *

Now that everything seemed in place again, I looked forward to the next three months and my new life in Tehran. I was curious about my new job, the people I would meet, and everything else to discover. I learned that the work week was from Saturday to Wednesday evening. Weekends began on Thursday morning and ended on Friday evening. Having a free Thursday and Friday weekend and working on Saturdays and Sundays felt different, strange, and extraordinary.

In the beginning, I needed to get used to it. I was tired when I got up on a Saturday and Sunday morning to go to work. Taking off two days in the middle of the week was even more awkward because I didn't feel I had the right to relax and didn't know what to do when stores were closed. Sitting alone in my tiny student apartment at the hostel, I realized how much I had been programmed into specific behaviors and patterns from my home country. My expectations, thoughts, and evaluations about good and evil need to be trained anew. It felt awkward, but I had to learn my life's new rules. I decided to learn, be curious, and enjoy my stay in Tehran.

My first day of work started with the next adventure. The new obstacle I faced: How would I get from the hostel in the south of Tehran to my new office up in the north? It sounded easy, but it was challenging if you couldn't even read the writing of the street signs, pronounce the street name, or speak the language to ask where to go. There were no Google Maps, GPS, or translation apps on a mobile phone. Those tools of today's society were not invented back then.

I was lost. The writing on all the street signs looked like beautiful artwork without any meaning to me. Fortunately, I had an English city map. How do you articulate yourself in the four-million-people city of Tehran or find your way when you can neither read nor speak so that people would understand you? Only the highly educated people of Tehran spoke English. Being a student of economics, I was puzzled. Ultimately, I had to walk from my hostel to the office using my city map. It took me more than two hours. I was exhausted; my feet were tired, but I finally arrived.

My American boss, who had lived in Tehran for many years, had expected that I would have trouble finding my way to the office. He took the time to explain the route I had to go or drive, but more importantly, he shared how public transport worked in Tehran.

"In Tehran, there is no public transportation like a bus or a tram you are used to having in Europe. You can't take a bus or a train. Shared taxis are public transportation. Shared taxis with other people will get you from A to B," he explained.

"What are shared taxis, and what do they look like? Do they have a sign on top of the car?" I asked.

"No, these are small cars, usually seating four to five people, including the driver. Nevertheless, you will see that six or seven people are placed in most cabs. They squeeze in because everyone is in a hurry and wants to reach their destination immediately. They get in without being shy or getting too close to anyone. And the driver will make more money per distance because everyone pays separately. Thus, the driver will cash four, five, and six times in the same direction. The more people in the cab, the better for him."

"Interesting. How do I know whether the taxi driver will also stop and pick me up? How do I know where the taxi is going? Does everyone in the taxi go in the same direction? Is there a stop sign, or where do they stop?"

"No, there are no designated pickup or drop-off spots for taxis. People wave their hands, and the taxicab stops if a seat is available. Nobody knows where the taxicab is going before hailing it, so you must tell him where you want to go. He either approves or declines. Even when a taxi seems fully occupied, the driver may still stop. You ask where he will be driving or shout the street name where you want to stop. He will confirm if he is driving to a nearby street or building. Then, you squeeze in."

"Okay, will the taxi driver always drive straight to the building where I wanna go, or do I have to change a taxi on certain corners where big streets are crossing?"

"Good question. I suggest switching taxis depending on the street you are waiting for. Most taxis take a certain route. They don't make extra turns for you. Sometimes, you must switch taxis. It's best always to have your city map to know where you are and not get lost."

"Oh wow, that sounds pretty complex. How do I inform a taxi driver that I am looking for a taxi ride? How do I stop a taxi?"

"You simply need to put up your arm and wave with your hand, like in New York City."

"I haven't been to New York City."

"You will figure it out. Just raise your arm and wave. The taxi will see you and stop immediately. Don't worry."

"Last question: How much money do I need to pay the taxi driver for a certain route?"

"He will tell you when to leave the car. You pay from where you are boarding to where you step out. After a while, you will know how much it will cost. It doesn't change. A flat rate is due for every trip from Street A to Street B within the city's inner circle. You say stop, give him the money, and get out."

"Okay . . ." I breathed. I was overwhelmed by memorizing all these instructions.

The first evening, I stood at the crossroads of two streets. My first challenge was finding a taxicab. Each car I saw passing me, driving back and forth, seemed to look alike. Unfortunately, there was no taxi sign on the roof, so there may not have been any taxis around.

I didn't see any taxi-like car going in either direction. It was getting dark, and I wanted to return to my hostel. I was not in the mood to walk back another two and a half hours. Nobody stopped. I put up my arm and started waving. One car stopped shortly after. I needed clarification and said the name of the street. The driver nodded his head and waited for me to board. I squeezed myself into the seats next to two other women. After thirty minutes of driving through Tehran, he yelled the name of my street and stopped. It was close to my hostel. I paid him and got out. I was proud and happy to have made it home safely.

Another big challenge was getting used to the pronunciation and reading the street names in Farsi. My city map was in English, and the street signs were in Farsi. In the beginning, I could not use either one of them. I had no orientation. I had to learn both the reading and the pronunciation. First, I made a list of street names, memorized them, and learned their pronunciation. Next, I drew my city map for the directions to the most important streets that would lead me to my destinations. Later, when I had a good sense of orientation, I put the names on the city map to figure out where I had to go.

I always arrived safely, although sometimes it took a little longer. I often stepped out on the wrong street and had to look for another taxi. Getting oriented in that vast city was quite a challenge. But it was a great way to explore and see many different parts of the town. I felt comfortable after a while.

My experience with shared taxi transportation also taught me much about Persian body language. Expressing a simple word like "no" or "yes" differs significantly from Europe or any other Western culture. If you want to say "no," you say "na," make a specific sibilant sound, and nod your head from the bottom up, not the top down. Suppose you agree or want to say "yes." You say "bala," shaking your head simultaneously. It's opposite to our body language, which initially brought me into confusing situations, especially with those taxi drivers. They stopped when they thought I said yes while shaking my head because I wanted to say no. They kept going and passed by if I wanted them to stop because I nodded.

"Hey, wait!"...But they couldn't understand or hear me.

Sometimes, I got impatient or even upset, and occasionally, I had to laugh. Observing myself and realizing how I and everyone around me have been conditioned in body language, unconsciously practicing cultural differences was weird. After a while, I moved comfortably in and out of taxis, proudly maneuvering myself in Tehran's horrific traffic. I would never drive a car by myself in that city. Someone once said driving in Tehran is even more dangerous than driving in Paris, France. I agreed, shaking my head.

*　*　*

The job at the market research company was quite exciting and compelling. I was privileged to work on a confidential project the Iranian Management School had requested. We had to find an answer to the most critical question for a country and its people: What is the import/export quota for all kinds of food and non-food products, specifically for the city of Tehran? In other words, how much food and what kind is in store for the Tehran population, and how long will it last? Or, in other words, what would be the time length in which the citizens of Tehran could be provided with food and water, i.e., in days, weeks, or months, if foreign governments impose a food embargo on the country?

We surveyed all food companies delivering to Tehran, both foreign and Iranian companies. I was privileged to interview international companies that sold food and beverages in Tehran. I asked them about their import/

export numbers on the most critical food categories: water, bread, meat, vegetables, fruits, and dairy products. We cross-checked and proved our results by interviewing international logistics companies. It was mind-blowing in every sense working on the project, interviewing people, and analyzing the results. It allowed me to meet many expats from Europe and the USA who are working in Tehran.

After four weeks, we finally had the results. They were shocking. Ten days. The city of Tehran could provide food for its four million people for, at most, ten days. After ten days, the people would start to starve. The city of Tehran and, consequently, the entire nation relied on foreign countries and companies to deliver food and beverages. Even the Iranian meat everyone favored—lamb and mutton—came from neighboring Iraq. The animals were raised in Iraq but then slaughtered right behind the border on the soil of Iran, thus labeled as Iranian lamb and mutton.

Being entirely dependent on other countries is dangerous for any country, its government, and its borders. When it comes to water and food, it could easily be blackmailed. Companies and countries that know those dependencies could take advantage of this weakness to dictate their prices or do even more harm.

The lack of investment in its food production industries, agriculture, farmers, and ranchers weakened Iran and its people. It counteracted and played against the Shah's strategy of opening the country to the world. It was the dark side the government wasn't expecting or aware of. Spreading the news of these results would create panic among the Iranian people. That's how seeds of indoctrination grow, and it is one of many explanations for public dissatisfaction and complaints, which is a breeding ground for rebellion and revolution. Thus, the research results had to be handled strictly confidentially.

* * *

After a week of living in the student hostel for women only, I was fed up. Taking a taxi every morning and evening, driving the long way to and from the office to the hostel, was annoying and expensive, too. Each night at 10:00 p.m., the student hostel for women locked their doors. Nobody could get in after 10:00 p.m., meaning I always had to return there in the early evening. I was missing out on social life and getting to know other students from different faculties and countries. It felt like living in prison again. And I missed my new German friends, Bob and Ellen.

I picked up the public phone and called them.

"When shall we pick you up at the hostel? Tomorrow?" Bob asked me right away after I said hello and my name. I had to laugh and didn't need to explain my situation. They knew already.

I was stunned and felt blessed. The next day, the family - Bob, Ellen, and their two sons—picked me up at the hostel. They were happy to see me, and I was delighted to see these great people again.

They welcomed me with open arms, which made me like them even more. I also loved having company now to share stories of my new life in Tehran and enjoying the beautiful home with a swimming pool.

I became part of their wonderful family life with regular meals, leisure time, and evening talks at the pool with a glass of wine.

One day, the family introduced me to their special Iranian friend and bodyguard, Mohsen, who was a few years older than me and regularly visited them. He was a bright and very handsome man. Tall, slender, athletic body, with black hair, black eyes, and a great, embracing smile. I was smitten and felt an immediate connection to him. A son of a wealthy Persian family, Mohsen studied business administration at the Iranian Management School and was almost finished with his master's degree. He loved being around the German family, which opened the door for him to the international world. In reverse, he opened the doors to critical governmental offices, people, and businesses, which was helpful to Bob. Mohsen wanted to visit Germany one day and was keen to learn our language.

Ellen and I became friends over time. Although twelve years older than me, she seemed happy to have found someone by her side whom she could talk to in her language. Bob worked very long hours, and sometimes, during the weekend, we spent a lot of time telling stories and talking about fashion and other girl topics. She shared her most intimate stories while we shopped or walked together. I listened and asked questions. She came from a small village near Frankfurt and got an education as a nurse practitioner. At a friend's party one day, she was introduced to Bob, who worked for a German company near Frankfurt.

Bob offered her a new world in Frankfurt, and they married a few years later. Their first son, Alexander, was born, and Oliver came two years later. Shortly after, Bob got an assignment to work for his German employer in Tehran. Both didn't need to think a second about the offer. They were bored living in the small, narrow-minded world of Germany. They couldn't see themselves getting old there. In addition, the salary was much higher, and the company paid extra for housing, cars, and schools, which made it even easier to decide to leave everything behind. They were happy to take the chance and moved to Tehran.

"That's my story," Ellen explained one afternoon. "We could not afford a house with a swimming pool like that if we would have stayed in Germany.

Although our life is great, I miss my friends over there. Over the years, taking care of the boys and spending most of the time by myself, I feel alone."

"I fully understand. It would be best if you started a social life. Why don't you become a member of a tennis club, and meet people there? Tennis seems to be the big thing here."

"Yes, that's what we already do. Bob and I go there to play tennis once a week. But it's hard to make friends on a deeper level. I don't trust the women there. These women are the wives of Bob's colleagues, and they gossip too much. They don't have anything else in their lives. Whatever I would tell them, Bob would know it the following day."

"Why would that be a problem?" I asked her curiously. What was she trying to tell me?

She didn't answer my question.

"So, what about you? Do you have a boyfriend in Germany? Why did you want to come here for three months?"

"I had a boyfriend, but we broke up. He already had another girlfriend, and after a while, I asked him to make a decision. He wanted to have us both at the same time. The other woman was more flexible for an open relationship, but I couldn't do that. He went back and forth for a while. But then he chose her at the end of the day. It was heartbreaking. Thus, I needed to escape."

"How long were you together?"

"Almost a year. Listen, I don't want to talk about that in more detail. It's too painful. I have come to Tehran to forget everything and start a new life again."

"Okay, I understand. I won't tell anyone, and I won't ask you again."

"Thank you. Appreciate it." I needed to rest and went to bed.

*　　*　　*

I was glad that Mohsen visited the following evening. I enjoyed talking to him, and from that day, Mohsen visited us every other day in the afternoon or evening. He picked me up to give me sightseeing tours, showing me all the great places in Tehran. He was proud to teach me everything about his country, people, lifestyle, and culture, founded in the first millennium BC, over four thousand years ago. It was the first time I had heard about Persepolis, the ancient city of Persia near Shiraz in the south of Iran. We talked for hours every time we met.

I remember one afternoon when we drove to a beautiful park with lavish green trees, lawns, flowers, and designed walkways. The air was fresh and cool. While walking through the park, he started talking about the great Persian poets Hafiz and Rumi, whose names I heard for the first time. We stopped at a water fountain, sat in the shade under an old tree, and listened to the sound of the water and the birds around us. Nobody said a word. It was peaceful and quiet. After a while, he took a little white book out of his pocket. It had an orange ornament framing the cover. The title was *Hafiz*.

"The little book contains some of the most essential poems written by Hafiz in Persian, typed together with the English translation. There is no better way to understand the Persian culture than reading the poems of Hafiz and Rumi," he explained. "Do you like poetry?"

"Yes, I do. I love reading all kinds of literature."

"Rumi wrote these poems seven hundred years ago. Can you imagine they are that old?" He was proud of his ancestors.

"I can't imagine that. It blows my mind thinking about the time since then." I was in awe.

To my surprise, Mohsen began reading Hafiz's first poem, "Love's Awakening."
I never heard someone reciting poems or reading from a book aloud just for me. Mohsen read it in Farsi first, and then the translation was written in old English.

It was a bittersweet poem about love.

"Love seemed at first an easy thing.
But ah! The brutal awakening."

I sensed he was talking about his own experiences. He must have had some sad memories. I could see and hear it in his voice, but I didn't dare to ask.

"Within life's caravanserai
What brief security have I,
When momentary, the bell doth cry
Bind on your loads; the hour is nigh!"

It was beautiful to listen to him. He continued reading, and I loved his voice. Time stood still while he recited Hafiz. Even the birds stopped talking and listened. I was falling.

"Do you like it?"

"Yes, it's so beautiful. I am very touched by the words. They are so true, even today. Timeless poetry."

"I hoped you would like them. Please take the book as a gift. I bought it for you."

"Gosh... that's so sweet. Thank you so much." I looked at him in awe.

"Nearby Shiraz, you can visit the tomb of Hafiz because he was born there. But you might never drive down there into the south. It's a two-day trip. But . . ." He smiled like a kid who had a surprise to offer. "I will show you the little pavilion they have built to honor Hafiz nearby!"

We walked through the beautiful park, passing couples sitting at the water of a small creek.

Suddenly, the park opened, and I saw a little pavilion built in a circle. It had several pillars supporting a French-style rooftop. Many young couples walked around and into Hafiz's memorial.

"How do you like it?"

"It's beautiful. I like it, especially since you have read that poem aloud. I have a special connection to this place now and will never forget it. I see what Hafiz means to you and all these people strolling around the pavilion."

"Yes, they hope for luck in their marriages. I am glad that you like it. There is one more special thing I want to show you. You will only find it here and in Shiraz. Do you see the guy with the colorful canary birds sitting on his arm?"

"Yes, I do. What is it all about? Why is he carrying these funny little birds? I know them."

"These birds are famous for giving prophecies by picking a Hafiz poem on paper from their hat, full of little notes. Couples who are in love and want to get married look for luck in their marriage by asking the bird to predict their future."

"Wow, that's amazing." I loved these sweet, colorful birdies. I had owned one myself many years before. "What must I do to get a birdie to pick up a pretty Hafiz poem?"

"While I will pay for it, you must consider a wish. Then, one canary will pick up a note with a love poem from Hafiz. You take it, read it, keep it, and don't tell anybody which poem you have received."

*   *   *

Over the weeks, Ellen and I had become friends. She taught me a lot about Persian food, especially spices and recipes. We bought groceries together, and I helped her cook dinner for the entire family.

"I am having an affair with another man, a German engineer," she told me one evening while we chopped vegetables for dinner.

"What? What did you say?" I was in disbelief.

"Yes, I met him at a reception at the German Iranian Chamber of Commerce several months ago. I fell in love with him and started an affair. Bob doesn't know anything about it."

I was shocked. My ideal world and perception of a perfect couple and family shattered.

"What would *you* do?" she asked me.

"What would *I* do?" I was amazed. "Truthfully, I would not even think about starting an affair with another man when I have my own family."

Painful memories of my mom having affairs and cheating on my dad came up. My dad worked in foreign countries, so we rarely saw him—maybe once a year for four weeks only. For the rest of the year, I remember other men in our house trying to play dad for my sister and me. I hated it and didn't like any of them. I usually disappeared in my room whenever she came home with her boyfriend. My parents got divorced finally because my dad had figured it out. He had hired a detective who showed him the photos confirming the evidence. The divorce, which involved a year of fighting between my parents, was one of the most hurtful experiences my sister and I had.

"Ellen, you have a responsibility. You have kids and must care for the family to keep it together. You need to stop this while nobody knows."

We immediately stopped our discussion because Bob came home with the two sons. I needed clarification.

A week later, I met Ellen for a coffee in the afternoon, continuing the discussion about her affair.

"Ellen, you are not independent; you are not a single woman without any responsibility aside from herself. You can't leave everything behind. I can do that, but not you." She looked at me with surprise.

"Life is not about yourself anymore. You have a family. Your way of living and decisions impact Bob and your kids. He might get over it and find another woman for a wife. But you will forever impact the lives of your sons and their perception of women who cheat on loved ones. They will lose trust in any relationship with a woman. Forever. You don't want that, do you? Bob is a rare example of a great guy. He deserves better than that."

I was upset. Her story triggered all those negative memories of my parent's divorce. Suddenly, Ellen seemed careless and selfish. I had hoped she would be more thoughtful than this.

And I didn't expect her to get me entangled in her love affair and trouble me with her marriage issues. It was not my business, and I liked Bob. From then on, I would lie to him to cover up for her. I hated lying to people I liked. My Tehran paradise was a façade that had become cracked. It was deeply disappointing.

"Yes, I agree, but I love the other one, too. The other one is so different from Bob. He takes care of me and appreciates me. My two boys will get older and leave the house one day. Then I will be all by myself. I won't have anything that will remain. That scares me."

"No, I don't think you deeply love the other man. You have a crush on him, that's all. It's an adventure with some new excitement in your life. You feel appreciated and seen by this man. You miss that in your marriage after being together for so many years. A secretive affair is always thrilling because it is a hidden and forbidden act in every culture."

Ellen looked at me in surprise. She didn't expect me to judge her.

"Your life has become boring. Having an affair is your way to escape your real life. You have a family, and the four of you live in a foreign country, far away from home. That's an even bigger responsibility for your family. How will you tell your sons you will leave them for a stranger? They would think that you don't love them anymore. Or would your lover take you with your two sons as a package? I doubt it. Your affair has no future because you love your sons and would never leave them. The affair is a dreamy, unrealistic, but egotistic piece of shit. Can you hear me?"

My voice became quite harsh and stern. My heart was pounding, but I had to tell Ellen, risking she would throw me out of the house.

"That's a tough response you are offering. I am surprised and disappointed. I expected more tolerance from you and had hoped you could help me decide. I had hoped you would understand my situation. What you are saying makes me feel guilty and ashamed."

"Did you understand what I was saying? You are not a victim, but everyone else will be if you continue doing what you do. You should indeed feel guilty about that, not about what I said. It's easy for me to see what you should decide, and I have said so plainly. Now, you must choose. You can trust me. I won't say anything to Bob because it's not my business, and I won't get between you."

We had dinner together. Ellen went into her room after we cleaned up the kitchen.

I entered the living room, where Bob sat at the bar. He had poured himself a glass of whiskey. I wondered whether he had heard what Ellen and I were discussing.

"Do you care for a whiskey?" he asked me.

"No, thank you. I can't drink that strong stuff. But I wouldn't say no to a glass of wine."

"Okay. So, what's up? How are your job and love life?" he asked me, smiling.

"My job is exciting, and other than that, I am having fun. I have recently met many people from all over Europe during several receptions at the German and British embassies. Meanwhile, we meet regularly at an international hotel where all international flight crews make a stopover, too. It's great talking to people from different European countries and the rest of the world. I have much more in common with them than I thought."

"What do you mean?"

"Well, it feels easier to connect with Europeans than with people in Iran. I don't have to think about whether somebody will understand my language or if my mannerisms, body language, or what I say bothers someone. I need more knowledge about Persian and Islamic culture and lifestyle. I have a Christian background. Thus, I must consider whether my behavior annoys someone from another religion."

"I understand. But you have already learned a lot; you speak basic Farsi, which helps you, too. You know that I like you a lot. If there is anything I can do for you, just let me know."

"Thank you, it's appreciated. That's very kind."

*　*　*

The next day, Mohsen came to visit. I was excited. He stood at the front door with a big smile. He was proud to show me around and help me get acquainted with his hometown. He picked me up in his white car, starting the next private sightseeing tour of Tehran. He drove me through the city, proudly presenting jaw-dropping archaeological treasures and monuments of his millennia-old culture. I was profoundly impressed.

Mohsen aimed to teach me everything necessary about his culture by looking behind the curtain and deeply understanding his country and heritage. He showed up every other day. He invited me to traditional Persian restaurants, and I indulged in Iranian food tasting. It was so different from what I was used to eating and cooking. The selection of various foreign restaurants was superb. I fell in love with Iranian food, cooked with great passion—delicious combinations like red cherries in rice or meat with yogurt and spices I had never seen or tasted before. I loved the mouthwatering traditional dishes with lamb or fresh fish. For the first time, I tasted their famous beluga caviar, served as a starter almost everywhere at any dinner place. Beluga caviar is from the sturgeon fish living in the Caspian Sea, a three-hour drive from Tehran.

Mohsen also invited me to accompany him to several private events at his friends' homes. As a European, I felt privileged and grateful to discover their beautiful culture, people, and lifestyle. It was unusual that a foreigner like me had the opportunity to look behind the doors of wealthy Iranian homes. It felt like discovering a secret world.

With Mohsen, I met some of Tehran's gorgeous and rich people, who were his friends. I got a glimpse of his culture, too. The outstanding hospitality of the Persian people that came from the core of their hearts deeply impressed me. Mohsen was one of Tehran's upper-ten-thousand club members, and I had the privilege to accompany him to family and friends' events. He introduced me to everyone at a party and never left me alone while talking to others. He was a real gentleman. I felt appreciated, comforted, taken care of, and very welcomed.

I remember when Mohsen invited me to a wedding reception at one of his friends' houses. The afternoon party was set in the garden of a palace-sized mansion.

The wealth and luxury of this reception took my breath away. It blew my mind. The mansion was nestled in a park, a perfectly designed garden with green lawns, flower beds, and giant trees. Little paths made of Belgian marble stones in red with white dots led to different water fountains surrounded by rare flowers. It looked like the gardens of Versailles near Paris. Gorgeous women and men were strolling around and enjoying themselves in seemingly heaven. The floors of the mansion were made of white Carrara marble. The walls of the dining hall and various living rooms were designed with specific patterns tessellated by actual gold, turquoise, and other precious gems. Chandeliers and different light sources topped by emeralds, sapphires, and rubies shined in competition with the hosts' and guests' jewelry and clothing. Breathtaking, beautiful. I stood there, looking around, speechless.

I felt like I was placed in my favorite book as a child, *The Stories of Thousand and One Nights*.

It was real, instead. I could touch it with my fingers. I had never seen anything like that before and have never seen something like that again until today.

Mohsen was laughing and excited, watching me walk around with big eyes and open mouth. I couldn't say a word. I was daunted and happy - all simultaneously.

Mohsen explained that the most precious and favorite flower that brings luck to a Persian is the gladiola (the name comes from the word "glad").

Gladiolas have tall, long stems and come in almost every color imaginable.

Gladiolas were placed indoors and outdoors in dozens of floor vases at this wedding reception. Breathtakingly stunning. After two hours of small talk and congratulating the bride and groom, Mohsen and I said goodbye and left. Because I was a stranger to the hosts, I could only expect to stay for a short time, but not for the dinner party. I felt sad for Mohsen because the groom was one of his best friends.

"Don't you want to stay and celebrate with them? I would understand, and it's okay with me. I can grab a taxi and go home on my own. I don't mind."

"Don't worry about me. It would be best not to leave this party alone. I care about you, and in our society, letting you go by yourself is perceived as impolite toward a woman. So, don't even think about it. But I appreciate your thoughts and consideration."

He grabbed my arm, and we left. I was impressed and felt comforted.

"It's okay for me and them also." He added.

"We have known each other for a long time. I told both of them I would bring you as a guest. I will meet them when they come back from their honeymoon. It's all good." He smiled at me.

I sighed. How could I not fall in love with him?

*　　*　　*

A week later, Mohsen called me at home one afternoon.

"I have a surprise for you."

"Hey, how are you doing?"

"Can you get dressed up, please? I want to show you Tehran's nightlife. I will pick you up in three hours at 6:00 p.m."

"Oh, okay. That's a surprise." I was happily excited and hung up.

Wow. He didn't even ask me whether I would have the time to spend the evening with him. He knew I would have stayed home because a decent woman in Iran would never be seen alone in Tehran's nightlife.

I ran into the bathroom to shower and get dressed. What should I wear? I needed to prepare for a date. The only nice piece I had with me was my short black dress. That was it. I didn't know whether this dress was even appropriate. I wish I had had the time to buy a new one. But the joy of spending the evening with him while not knowing where to go was compelling, exciting, and irresistible.

He always picked me up in his white car, parking in front of Bob's and Ellen's house. When I opened the door, I had to hold my breath. He looked fantastic with his athlete's body, black eyes, black hair, white dinner jacket, and bow tie.

"Hi…" I coughed.

"Good evening, my love… You look adorable in your little black dress."

He opened the door to his car with a big smile and an intense look at me. I could tell he liked what he saw, and I got goosebumps. I took my seat in the car. He closed the door and walked around to take the driver's seat.

Handsome men always make me nervous; sometimes, my mind goes blank. I am a shy woman when I am in private. I couldn't look him in his eyes and lowered my gaze. He started the car engine. I tried to act cool, being an elegant, serene woman.

"Where are we going?" My voice was still scratchy.

"It's called dinner dancing and is performed by live bands from the USA and the UK who play modern, international music. I am sure you will like it."

"Okay . . ." I had no idea what Mohsen was talking about.

He turned and looked at me, somehow worried.

"Are you okay? Are you sure you want to go? I didn't even ask you…."

"Yes, I am." I cleared my throat. "I've got a little green frog in my throat, which will disappear soon," I smiled back. "So, how is the program set up tonight? Is it like we eat first and then go to a disco club for dancing later? That's how we spend an evening in Germany."

He laughed.

"No, no, it is much easier and more comfortable. It's all set up simultaneously, usually in one big restaurant with a dance floor in the middle and tables around, seating eight people each. A big band will be playing live music all evening. The setting is quite elegant. Dinner dancing has become very popular, especially among expats."

"I am excited. I have no idea what it will look like, but I am looking forward to it."

We drove to the Hotel Intercontinental, a well-known place for travelers and business people worldwide. The main restaurant, which offered "Dinner Dancing," was on the rooftop, with tall windows from top to bottom and 360 degrees around, offering a great view of Tehran and its city lights during the night.

I was in awe. Men and women were elegantly dressed up. Mohsen had made a reservation for us, sitting at a table with three more couples. We introduced ourselves, and the party began.

"So, how does this work?"

"We will eat and dance, all at the same time. The band plays all night with only one break. Whenever they play a song you like, we dance on the dance floor."

"Sounds easy. I can handle that." I smiled at him.

*   *   *

Mohsen laughed and ordered a bottle of champagne and the famous Beluga caviar as an appetizer.

The band started to play, and I began to relax, enjoying the champagne, the setting, and the people around me; we were making small talk. Everyone was in a great mood. The energy was lovely and easy. Whenever I chewed something delicious in my mouth, Mohsen asked me to dance. He was very confident. He knew what he wanted. When he loved a song, he would grab my hand, and we would dance. Often, we would dance for two or three songs in a row. I realized these were the only moments he could pull me closer to himself in public. Thus, we would respect the rules for not being a couple officially or getting me into trouble publicly.

I liked it a lot. I was in heaven.

I couldn't get enough. Returning to our table, often out of breath from dancing, we continued eating the food on our plates that had already gotten cold. That was okay, too. Food was not important any longer.

Since that day, dinner dancing has become my favorite entertainment program.

Late into the night, Mohsen drove me to Bob and Ellen's home. He stopped the car in front of their house, walked around the car, and opened my door again, offering his hand to help me out. He was a gentleman with perfect manners and a subtle seducer, too. I wondered whether he knew how attractive he was because he was also humble, respectful, and down-to-earth at the same time.

We were standing in front of the gate and looked at each other. I had too much champagne and felt like a spoiled princess walking on clouds.

"Thank you so much for this awesome evening. I have had so much fun. The music, food, setting, and everything else were perfect with you. Thank you so much for this unforgettable evening."

I was all smiles.

"*You* are perfect, Gabby, and you are very welcome."

My heart melted. "Thank you. That's very sweet."

I lowered my gaze. *Say something,* my inner voice commanded.

But my mind needed clarification. What shall I say? Something tender or a compliment? What? I didn't know. I had no idea. My mind was swirling and then went blank again. I was shaking my head.

"Well then, goodnight, Mohsen."

"Good night, my love." He pulled me close to his chest and kissed me goodnight for the first time.

*　*　*

I met Ellen the next day.

"What did you do last night? Bob saw you all dressed up and leaving the house."

"Mohsen took me to dinner-dancing at the Intercontinental. It was simply enchanting."

"That was very sweet of him. You look so happy. Is there something going on between you and Mohsen?" she asked.

"Maybe… I don't know." I got myself a cup of coffee.

"You know that he is a Muslim, and you're a Christian. I don't think it's a good match."

"It's far too early to think about a match."

I was disappointed to hear that. I knew Ellen could be correct, but who knew? I hoped the story between Mohsen and me would turn out as well as it had started.

"We were having a great time. That's all. What about you? Have you decided about your affair? Are you going to end it?" I harshly responded, distracting her from my story.

"Maybe. I don't know."

She didn't like to talk about it. She knew that I would not support her having an affair.

"You better decide as soon as possible. Bob will figure it out one day and then leave you. That will make things worse for you. Do you want that?"

"What do you mean?"

"You will be found guilty in court because you were cheating on Bob, thus perceived to be destroying the family. You will be guilty as the cause of the divorce. That's German family law. That means you won't have the right to see your sons anymore, nor will you get any monthly payments as part of a settlement agreement."

"How do you know all of that?"

"My mom had an affair, and my dad found out and filed for divorce. As a result, she didn't get any money from him for her personal needs. She received a monthly payment to cover my and my sister's expenses. She had to find a job for the first time in her life and had to start all over again, a new life after being married for thirteen years. My mother, sister and I moved from a thirty-five-hundred-square-foot bungalow with a ten-thousand-square-foot garden to an eight-hundred-square-foot mini-apartment without a garden. We had to give away our beloved German Shepherd, which was the most painful thing I had to endure. My sister and I were old enough to decide to stay with our mom. But your sons are too young to decide. They will stay here in Tehran with Bob."

She fell silent.

"Look around. You will lose everything: your kids, your house with the garden and swimming pool, your friends, and any other connections because you will be the one who created all the mess. You better think twice, Ellen."

I got emotional. We had exchanged roles. It seemed I had become the older one giving Ellen advice, although I was much younger.

*   *   *

In mid-August, I took a one-week trip south into the desert with my fellow international students from AIESEC. The state of Iran is the size of Germany and France, so it's at least a two-day trip by bus to the Persian Gulf. We stopped in Isfahan and Qom, the holy cities in Iran. Mosques with golden domes and mosaics made of turquoise stones matching the blue sky's color dominated the city's view. Impressive.

The first time we entered a mosque, I recognized a change in the behavior of my fellow female Muslim colleagues from AIESEC. They didn't want to be approached by a question about the mosque or distracted in any way. Suddenly, they were gazing at me with a piercing look that made me feel that I was the enemy. I felt very uncomfortable. I understood, left the mosque immediately, and waited outside. It took an hour until they came out with a big smile and chatted as if nothing had happened.

It dawned on me. I was a Christian. This must have been the reason for their behavior when I was in the mosque with them. A fellow Iranian student told me that Christians and Jews are not welcome to visit a mosque. Surprisingly, he told me that Iranians and Germans have much in common, like history and heritage. The name "Iran" derived from "Eran" or "Eran Shahr" approximately a thousand years ago, which later changed into "airy-nam" and "Aryan" and has been transformed into "Iran" today.

"Farsi is an Indo-European language; thus, it does not have an Arabic historical background, but a German one."

I was confused and confounded. I had no idea. I had to learn more.

Our trip took us through the desert. We had a stopover and visited the ancient city of the Persians, Persepolis, built in 520 BC and destroyed in 330 BC by Alexander the Great. I couldn't imagine the architectural layout; the remaining ancient stones and pillars were that old. We finally arrived in Shiraz.

Shiraz is quite close to Persepolis, a city in the desert near the Persian Gulf. It is the place where the great poet Hafiz was born and died. He wrote his poems here. I was daydreaming about Mohsen, our wonderful gatherings, him reading Hafiz poems to me, and the little prophetic canary birdies in the park. All had left footprints in my heart.

Shiraz is also well-known as the City of Roses. Sidewalks, parks, and gardens are planted with roses everywhere. The dominant scent of the entire city was the fragrance of blooming roses. I was excited and loved the city from the first moment I arrived.

Mohsen told me that water is the most precious resource in the desert. Shiraz had built many small, blue-tiled water channels along the streets and gardens to preserve those roses. These channels deliver water for all plants right in the middle of the desert. The sound of fresh water bubbling and rippling was everywhere. Shiraz's wealth is revealed through these many water channels and rose plants.

After two days of discovering the city and visiting its popular sightseeing spots, including the Hafiz monument, we left Shiraz and drove back to Tehran.

Iran is a beautiful country with breathtaking diversity, beauty, nature, ancient history, ancient culture, and lovely people. I traveled to the desert in the south and also took a trip to the snowcapped Elburz Mountains and tropic-like vegetation at the Caspian Sea in the north, all within a few hours' drive from Tehran. Iran, in all its facets and people, had impressed me deeply. I was hooked. It seemed that I had arrived in paradise. I had an exciting job, was spoiled living with my German hosts in a beautiful house with a swimming pool, and the cherry on top was my friendship with Mohsen.

*　*　*

I became even more deeply acquainted with Tehran after meeting several Europeans at one of the international events, usually thrown by the British Consulate or the German Chamber of Commerce. The guests were expats from Germany, the UK, and the Netherlands. They worked for European companies in the logistics or food industries. I often ran into the same group of people at these events. A small clique of like-minded people asked me to hang out with them at the swimming pool of one of the international hotels. It was a lovely place where most of the flight crews from various airlines had a stopover. The guys liked it so much because of the pretty flight attendants at the pool bar.

We met there regularly. Once a week, on Thursday afternoons, we heralded the weekend taking place. Some days, our hang-out gang grew to fifteen people. These men from the Netherlands and Germany were like playful kids, having nothing on their minds but making fun of others. I remember being at the pool one afternoon, sitting in one of the Cabanas, chatting, drinking cocktails, and laughing. After a while, I got tired and decided to nap on one of the sun loungers. While I was falling asleep, I heard voices quietly chatting. I felt very comfortable. Then, their voices stopped and went silent. For a minute, I wondered why, but I didn't care much.

Two guys must have walked over to me on their tiptoes. I couldn't hear anything, but I felt their energy and presence. Before I could open my eyes, one guy grabbed my feet and the other under my arms. I had no chance to break free, although I was screaming, fighting, and laughing in surprise. They lifted, swayed, and threw me into the swimming pool. Everyone had fun watching that nasty game and laughed. I was shocked by the cold water, but I was awake immediately. Napping was the wrong idea. The two guys helped me out of the pool and charmingly offered me a drink as an apology. I was somehow intrigued by why they chose me. Maybe they knew I wouldn't be mad at them because we had become buddies. They wanted attention from the rest of the crowd, being the center of entertainment. They played a trick on me, and I was the victim. I had to laugh, too. For sure, it was the first and last time I took a nap at the hotel swimming pool.

We had the time of our lives and were always looking at the bright side. But besides all that fun, there was Mohsen. He had made his way straight into my heart from the first moment.

Ever since Ellen had mentioned that he was Muslim and from a wealthy, very conservative Persian family, I wondered whether our different cultures and religions would get in the way of a joint future. If so, it would be a reason I could accept because I was convinced that love alone would not help us manage our cultural differences successfully in the long run.

And yet, I trusted that he would find a way to overcome the differences if he wanted to. I seriously considered staying in Tehran, finishing my studies, and getting my master's degree at the Iranian Management School of Business in Tehran if only to spend more time with him.

*   *   *

"What's the story with Mohsen?" Bob asked me one evening while having another whiskey and sitting at the bar in the living room. Ellen had already disappeared into her bedroom.

"I see that he likes you. Otherwise, he wouldn't show up every other day. He didn't do that before you came into our house. Back then, he visited us only once a week, rarely twice a week. Now, it's different. Even when Mohsen can't make it to stop by, he calls. He's offering more support than I need. I assume he is doing that because he wants to know how *you* are doing and to have a reason to stop by and see you. He is a gentleman. "

"Yes, I know. It's very kind of Mohsen; he cares so much about us. I am trying to figure out the story between Mohsen and me. I also have met some great people from Europe. We are having a blast. We hang out at an international hotel once a week."

"Does Mohsen know?"

"Yes, I asked him to join us, but he rejected. It would be a good idea to meet more Europeans. Hmm… Maybe he doesn't like the European lifestyle. And, if he doesn't like me being around other people, he should tell me. We would need to talk about this."

"He wouldn't tell you. He adores you and has much respect for you. It would never occur to him to tell you what to do or not to do."

"Okay, but he should let me know if he wants more than a friendship. I have fallen in love with him. But I won't wait forever because my flight back to Germany will leave in six weeks. I can extend my stay till the end of the year, but that would be up to him to ask. I have already considered continuing my studies and finishing my master's degree at the Iranian Management School in Tehran."

I sighed.

"I wish he was one of the European men I've met."

"But then he wouldn't be the man you fell in love with," Bob commented with a knowing glance. He was a wise man.

"You are right . . . as always." I laughed.

*　　*　　*

Bob, Ellen, and their two sons left the house for a trip the following weekend. They wanted to visit the tropical landscape and beaches of the Caspian Sea, which was only a few hours' drive from Tehran, passing the Elburz Mountains. I promised to house-sit. I was happy to do that for them, too. They had done so much for me, and I wanted to do something in return for their hospitality.

It was the first time I got to enjoy the entire place alone. It was tranquil without them; I felt a little anxious and awkward. In the evening, I ate dinner and turned on the TV. I barely understood a word, zipping through the channels only to turn it off finally. I wandered around, looking for something to read. I found some novels besides the technical books from Bob. It was indeed a dull life without people around that I liked. I went to bed early.

The following day, I woke up fully refreshed. The first thing I wanted to do was go for a swim. I love the fresh air in the morning, the silent sound of a quiet sleeping city, and the birds happily starting their day. I was doing my sixth or seventh lap in the swimming pool when the phone rang in the living room. I was excited. I was sure it would be Mohsen. The weekend may not become as dull as it had started yesterday.

I tried to swim as fast as possible to escape the pool. It seemed to take forever, but I got out and ran into the living room. I was wet, dripping water all over. When I entered the living room, which had a granite stone floor, I slipped and fell on the edge of the coffee table, striking my ribcage.

"Ohoho, oh my goodness, shit, that hurt."

I could hardly breathe, and the pain in my ribcage was terrible. I grabbed the phone, but the ringing had stopped. He had already hung up. I felt stupid to run to the phone instead of taking my time. He surely would call again after a while. The pain in my ribcage was awful, and it felt like I was choking. After I caught my breath again, I walked out to the terrace to get my towel.

Then, I saw them—an invasion of quite giant ants walking through the wooden frame at the bottom of the terrace door straight into the living room. Within seconds, thousands of ants quickly conquered the entire floor before me.

"Where are my shoes?" I yelled to nobody.

I got chills. I searched the terrace for my shoes, put them on, and grabbed my towel as fast as I could with what I assumed was a broken rib. Then, I entered the house, jumping over the thousands of ants already marching into the living room. Their goal was definitely to find the kitchen, searching for yummy food.

"Damn… Where is the bug control spray or anything against ants?" I asked out loud.

Ellen had shown me, but I needed help remembering. The pain in my ribcage stopped me from thinking clearly. I ran back into the living room to check the situation. Meanwhile, an army of ants had already reached the Persian carpet, covering the room's central area, starting at the front door of the living room. I didn't want them to go any further.

"The only time I had the privilege to be alone at the place is now messed up by ants and a broken ribcage," I said, rolling my eyes.

I got angry but was in trouble and had to solve my ant problem quickly. I had to conquer an attack of thousands of ants who would destroy all furniture first and then the house. I thought about drowning them in the water, but somehow, I remembered my dad telling me ants can swim.

Damn. There were too many ants. I was terrified and panicked, desperately trying to find a solution. I ran back into the kitchen three times and opened every door of the cabinets to search for anti-ant spray. I couldn't find anything similar. I knew it must be somewhere.

Then, I had an idea to prevent these guys from taking control of the living room, furniture, and carpets, and marched into the kitchen to find food in the pantry. When I walked back into the living room, my eyes caught some coasters stacked on top of the bar, which were made from paperboard. I took them all, bending each in half as fast as possible. I set one half on fire with a lighter in the bar. Then, I placed one next to the other, building a firewall of twenty to thirty burning coasters on the carpet and all areas they had already conquered. I had to stop them from walking farther into the room. It worked. I watched them become confused, pacing back and forth to the side, wondering whether they could pass between the fire towers to continue their march.

"You guys stop!" I yelled as if they could hear me and would follow my orders. I was outraged, even furious, and immediately burned the most aggressive ones trying to make their way between the coasters. I kept the dead ants lying there as a warning symbol for all others. And finally, after eternal minutes, they stopped marching. They seemed to understand.

I ran to the bathroom and returned to the kitchen, finally finding the bug spray. It was in the pantry as usual, but I couldn't see clearly in my panic mode. I walked back into the living room, relieved. The ants were still confused; some were courageous and had walked between the fire pillars. I killed them first and then all the others. Then, I sprayed the wooden doorframe to the terrace and searched for the hole they had walked through. I saw several again following their brothers and sisters. They had no idea what they were walking into. No ant would ever walk into this house again for the rest of my life. I was destined to fulfill my mission. I felt terrible, but I had no choice: them or me.

After finishing my mission, I cleaned up the mess in the living room. I was still wearing my wet swimsuit, and the pain in my ribcage returned. While I was fighting the ants, I didn't feel anything. Meanwhile, it was lunchtime. The phone rang again, but I didn't pick up. I had already had enough excitement for the day. I was exhausted, and my ribcage hurt terribly. I had a hard time breathing. I must have broken one of my ribs when I fell on the edge of that coffee table. I locked all doors, went to bed, and napped till late afternoon until Bob, Ellen, and their sons returned from their trip.

"What happened? You look so pale."

"Well, I had an extraordinary day today. I was fighting for the survival of your house, and I managed to survive the attack of thousands of ants myself. I won, and they are all sitting in ant heaven now watching us, but I guess I have a broken rib."

"Oh my God, sit down! Have a glass of wine. Tell us what happened. What have these ants done to you? They broke your ribs?"

I had to laugh, which created more pain in my ribcage. The entire family sat around me, listening in awe to my adventure and what I had done to rescue their home. The burned coasters and some dead ants were my proof of evidence.

"You are a smart lady. I am glad you were in the house while we were gone." Bob emphasized.

"We know these aggressive ants. We have met them several times, too. They would have taken over the entire house if you had not been here. We would have been in real trouble. The ants had no idea that you were there to fight them and that you would stop them as the guardian of the house. Thank you so much. That was awesome. You are the heroine."

"It was my pleasure," I replied, jaded.

"Let's go out for dinner and celebrate the day. We will tell you about our experiences at the Caspian Sea, which were much nicer."

We left for dinner at a local Persian restaurant nearby.

*　　*　　*

In August, several political uprisings and attacks started occurring in other cities in Iran. We watched the news on TV the following days, but we did not realize how serious it could also become for Tehran. We didn't think much about bomb attacks. They were too far away. We had a good life.

Political discussions in public were never recommended, even forbidden. Everyone feared the Shah's secret service, the SAVAK, which seemed to be listening if someone criticized the Shah. So, we refrained from speaking about what we saw on TV. We lived in a bubble, not knowing what was going on outside. Life went on as usual. We were not concerned. But without a doubt, the attacks came closer.

We didn't anticipate that the Iranian people would be affected by the idea of an Islamic revolution. History books say that BBC London and Paris radio stations supported Ayatollah Khomeini's political views and speeches by broadcasting them live weekly. The anger of the Iranian people against the Shah's regime grew over time. In addition to many other reasons I am not fond of, their rage was incited by the Revolution Council and directed against Western values and lifestyle, which the Shah represented. For sure, foreigners from Western countries and cultures working and living in Tehran were perceived as the enemy. The danger of being attacked grew.

What next? Nobody could have known. I will never forget what happened to me in the upcoming weeks.

My careless, luxurious life in Tehran radically changed at the beginning of September. I was invited with two other international students on a weekend trip to visit the parents of an Iranian student. Karim asked us to spend the weekend with him and his family at their beautiful estate in the country. He picked us up in his Range Rover in downtown Tehran, and together, we drove to their ranch, which was about two hours outside of Tehran. We enjoyed the legendary Iranian hospitality and food, played tennis at their tennis court, and spent time with their horses, all part of the estate. It was peaceful. We lived in comfort.

On Friday, September 8, 1978, we drove back to Tehran. We took the main highway, the Grand Boulevard, toward the famous city gate, the Shahyad monument (today, it is Azadi Tower), and the Shahyad Square. We got stuck in a traffic jam several miles before we reached the memorial.

"We should have started earlier. I'm going to be late to the meeting." I was worried.

"Yes, but I can't help it. Unfortunately, there is no other way because this is the only main street that leads into the city," Karim explained.

After waiting about fifteen minutes, squeezed between cars, trucks, and motorcycles, Karim got out of his car.

"I will check what is happening. Please do not get out of curiosity and don't follow me. That's important, especially for you, Gabby. As a woman, you must stay in the car—no matter what happens!"

"Okay. What is going on? Maybe an accident?"

I remained seated in the car's front seat without being concerned. Two guys from the UK were sitting in the back.

After about an endless ten minutes, Karim rushed back, got in his driver's seat, looked at me, and commanded in a harsh tone:

"Go down, completely, including your head! Hide in the footwell and cover yourself up!"

"Excuse me? What?" I looked at him with a confused smile.

"Get down, immediately!" he yelled at me.

"Take your sweater or a scarf and cover up your head. I don't want you to be seen...".

"WHAT?"

I looked at him in fear, fighting back my tears. I hated it when someone yelled at me. Without saying another word, I followed his instructions. My heart was pounding, and my hands were shaking. I could hardly breathe. My body realized that I was in severe danger. I was scared to death. I knew he was serious.

He moved his car back and forth to make a U-turn, turned around, and drove back to his parents' country house. On the way, he told us what had happened in downtown Tehran. There had been a violent demonstration against the regime of the Shah, and many people were killed. It was the beginning of the Islamic Revolution, which took over the Iranian government. Rumors said that the Shah and his family had already left Tehran. None of us had an idea about the violence and murders that had happened in the city. It would change everyone's lives from that moment, including mine.

While driving back to Karim's family estate, I thought about Ellen, Bob, the kids, Mohsen, and my boss. They were probably wondering what had happened to me. I wanted to call any one of them and tell them where I was.

"No, not possible. The landlines are cut off."

Since Bob and Ellen knew I had spent the weekend in the countryside, so they would undoubtedly be concerned about me. I was also worried about whether they survived the violence in downtown Tehran. I was trapped, and it dawned on me that our lives were at stake. I was sure that my family and friends in Germany were worried, too. They must have learned about the revolution on TV but had no chance or way to contact me.

Karim drove us back to Tehran one week after the city had calmed down due to martial law and curfew hours. Now, I was sitting in the back seat of the Range Rover, entirely covered in a black chador I got from his sister. The closer we got to the city, the more we saw destroyed streets and shattered houses. Bullet holes from machine guns covered the walls. Some buildings were leveled. Only ruins remained. We passed military police with machine guns at their fingertips who were controlling cars, trucks, men and women, and even children.

One military patrol stopped us. We had to leave the Range Rover and put our hands in the air. They pointed their guns directly at each one of us. These guys were relatively young with wild-looking eyes and seemed determined to kill immediately. I didn't move, and I didn't breathe at all. I was frozen in fear of death. Karim explained that we were dear relatives visiting him and his family. They looked at me. Instinctively, I humbly bowed and did not look back into their eyes. I was safe because I had three men accompanying me. Karim must have said something that made sure that we could continue. Thank God we could go. We were relieved.

Initially, the revolution wasn't recognizable as an Islamic revolution, a jihad. The rebels' focus was fighting against the Shah, first and foremost against his government and the secret service (SAVAK). As I learned and read later, riots began on the Day of the Constitution, August 8, when the Shah announced democratic reforms and free elections.

"This is a new chapter in the history of our country. ... We will have the same freedom as in Europe, and the limits of freedom in Iran will not be different from those in Europe. ... That is, there will be parties, peaceful and unarmed parties. We will have freedom of speech and the press based on a new press law, which we will formulate based on the model of free world press laws. The upcoming elections will be completely free. Everyone has the right to vote, and each vote will count. But it must be clear that no nation that calls itself democratic can tolerate fights, violence, provocations, and lawlessness."

Despite this announcement, new protests followed soon. The Iranian people didn't believe him. Rebels stormed the Shah Abbas Hotel in Isfahan and set it on fire, a former caravansary that had become one of Iran's finest hotels. Islamists attacked cinemas, stores selling alcohol, banks, and government buildings. A bomb blew up a well-known tourist restaurant in Tehran. The bomb killed many people, primarily foreign visitors and tourists. The Shah and the SAVAK were accused of being initiators.

The Shah continued, "Myself, the national-minded Iranians, and the army will not allow Iran to fall into the hands of foreign agents." He suspected an alliance between the USA and Russia was supporting the Islamic rebels to take over his country.

A blaze was set in a large cinema in Abadan, murdering four hundred men, women, and children. It was publicly blamed on the Shah and his government. His words caused even more rage and desire to seek revenge against the monarchy. The rebel's tactics worked. The number of people who turned their back on the Shah and his government increased. Violent attacks continued in Qom and Mashhad, the centers of Islam in Iran. More attacks spread like wildfire to Shiraz, accompanied and fueled by the propaganda of the revolutionists.

The Shah and his family were Muslims, too. Who was behind all of it? History books say students initiated the revolution, ultimately leading to the Shah's fall and his government.

Many international people in Tehran who had lived there for years wondered and shook their heads in disbelief. "Could a handful of students defeat a monarchy plus an entire government, all military and secret service?" This could not have been possible without the help of the military and foreign countries.

Four weeks later, September 8, 1978, became a grieving day for the people in Iran because too many had died. Since then, the date has been called Black Friday. The Islamic Revolution that had started changed the entire country, and the shootings didn't end. Consequently, martial law was imposed on all cities in Iran to keep the situation under control and avoid escalation. Martial law means the military takes over and defines the rules for everyone. A strict curfew from 8:00 p.m. to 6:00 a.m. was commanded. Nobody was allowed to be seen on the street during the curfew, or they would be shot dead immediately without explanation or discussion.

It was also the beginning of a civil war against all people from Western countries and cultures, represented mainly by Americans and Europeans living in Tehran. It was a civil war against Christians and Jews and everything that comes with those identities, too—a jihad. We, people from Western cultures, English-speaking and white-skinned, had become the embodiment of the enemy, regardless of nationality. We met every criterion for their hate and knew that we would have to face punishment or death when caught by fanatic Islamists. Hatred against foreigners increased among Iranians. We were terrified. As an English-speaking, blonde woman with blue eyes, I was perceived as an American. I was scared to death.

Gatherings on the street, in parks, or in pubs were banned, and restaurants, cinemas, and nightclubs were closed. Playing Western music, drinking alcohol, or any other form of entertainment was forbidden. Women were no longer allowed to work or be seen on the street without male company. Public life died suddenly and entirely.

Tehran became silent, except for the sounds of shootings and bombings. Connecting to and meeting my European friends had become a nightmare. Communication was cut off; no landline worked anymore. We didn't have any internet or smartphones at that time. We had to plan our gatherings carefully, including how to return home before 8:00 p.m. Usually, we started meeting around 4:00 p.m. and left the place where we met around 7:00 p.m. at the absolute latest.

We met not to party but to gather and not feel alone in the war zone. We wanted to find some community of Europeans, share what was going on, the latest news, and learn what to pay attention to. We also wanted to avoid getting into the danger zone of curfew hours. We met by making appointments using word of mouth or phones when connected. We were shut off from the rest of the world.

For us, Tehran had turned into a nightmare. It was devastating. Electricity was down every night, at home and in public. We lit candles and heard the shootings, even during the night. People were perpetually on edge, drained from having to grieve dead relatives and still fearful for their own lives, and yet, protests continued despite being forbidden. It seemed they were not afraid anymore.

From that day, all women had to be fully covered in public, hiding their Western dress. Some wore a black chador, and some wore a burqa, fully covering up their face. I wore a chador when I left the house or office. Wearing a scarf covering the hair and hairline was not enough. I had to wear a black chador or a black burqa. It was commanded that women had to follow the strict rules of Islam, written in the series of the Koran. Being seen unveiled in public was forbidden, and severely punished when caught. I heard some women were arrested for not following the new law correctly. Women were also not allowed to walk on the street without a man, and thus, every woman had to be accompanied by a man. A woman alone, even two women alone, would endanger herself or themselves, as they would be perceived as not honorable and thus breaking the new rules. I was covered up but unprotected by a man when making my way to get groceries, one shot away from being killed—my daily fear.

Over the weeks, more and more buildings inhabited by Western companies were attacked. Our favorite international hotel in Tehran, where Europeans met weekly together with the airline flight attendants, was bombed two weeks after I was thrown into the swimming pool by my fellow buddies as a funny joke. We got the message late in the morning when we planned to meet there in the afternoon. We were shocked to realize that some of our airline friends were killed. We would have been among them if the terrorists had decided to bomb the hotel in the afternoon instead. According to the Islamists, our hotel was the symbol of sin.

*   *   *

Mohsen somehow disappeared the day the revolution started on September 8th. I wanted to know where he was and what had happened to him. I was seriously concerned.

"What is going on with Mohsen?" I asked Bob. "Why is he not showing up anymore? Is he okay? Do you have any information about or from him?"

"I don't know. I talked to Mohsen on the phone a couple of days ago. He seems all right."

"What did he say? Was he asking for me?"

"Yes, he wanted to know whether you could escape last week's turmoil and chaos. He asked many questions about you and us and what we plan to do now."

"Okay. Did you tell Mohsen what happened to me?"

"Yes, I did. He is worried about you. Even if he wants to, he won't be able to help you in this situation. Otherwise, he and his family will get in trouble with the police or military."

"Why?" I didn't get it.

"It's because we are Europeans from a Western culture and lifestyle. That's an evil, wrong lifestyle in the perception of the conservative Islamists. That's why they wanted the fall of the Shah and the monarchy. We are representing that part of the world. Thus, every one of us is an enemy per se, too."

"Yes, I understand. But Mohsen knows us very well. He could tell that we were different. He could defend and help if some Iranian Islamists would want to kill us."

"No, he cannot. In doing so, he would also be chased. He would be a traitor in their perception. He would endanger not only his own life but that of his parents, siblings, cousins, his entire family. He would bring shame onto his family in the eyes of everyone around them, too. Do you understand? He can't, and he would never do that."

"Is it that bad? Is the hatred against foreigners that strong that they would kill Iranians, their people, even?"

"Yes, it is. It will become even stronger. Ultimately, it's all about the difference in values, how to live your life in God's faith, being either Christian or Jew, or being a Muslim living and practicing the values and rules of Islam."

When I asked some of my Muslim student friends from the university, they confirmed what Bob was trying to tell me. They knew what would likely happen in the upcoming weeks and months, foremost against foreigners.

"You have to leave the country immediately," Mohsen insisted when he visited us several days later. In doing so, he was at significant risk, too.

He seemed deeply concerned about us, Bob, Ellen, and me. He was a Muslim and knew what could happen in the worst case. No one could promise to get us out of Iran alive. No guarantee for safety or departure was given anymore, even with a booked flight back home. Every identified foreigner would be chased. The revolution had become a brutal war against non-Islamic people, the perceived enemies in the country. As a white Christian from Europe who spoke English, my chances of surviving this civil war were meager.

"What do you want me to do? I cannot leave the country just like that. I cannot afford to pay for one of these overpriced flights to get out earlier than planned. Everything else is overbooked." I told Mohsen later when we spoke on the phone.

" Every Western foreigner wants to leave the city as soon as possible. I wanted to reschedule my flight, but all flights out of Tehran are fully booked or overbooked every day for the next several weeks."

Mohsen didn't reply; there was silence on the other end of the line. He expected the phone to be hacked and wiretapped.

"Ticket prices have increased drastically. For people with enough money, it is quite easy to leave. I cannot afford to pay these huge prices to get out earlier. I must take my regularly booked flight, which is supposed to leave in mid-October. That means I must stay another four weeks, trapped in this jihad against Christians and Jews."

He didn't reply but listened.

"What do you think? I could rent a car and drive home by myself. It would be a long trip, but at least I could leave the country."

I was thinking out loud, and I was deeply hurt that he wanted me to leave the country. He couldn't help me this time.

I didn't reveal to him or say anything, but my heart was aching, and I started to cry silently. Tears rolled down my face. I wanted to stay with him, but I also knew that it was impossible. For the first time, I realized our cultural and religious differences were chasms apart. Ellen had been right when she tried to warn me several weeks ago.

"No, don't do that. Don't rent a car and drive back all alone. Driving without any male bodyguard, you won't even make it to the border of Iraq. They will spot you and kill you."

"What? What will happen to me? Am I imprisoned in this country? I am a free human being. Nobody can or should tell me what to do!"

"Yes, they can, and they will because you are a woman, and, secondly, you are a Christian from the Western world. These are your problems now. Don't neglect it or try to fight it. They will kill you immediately. Maybe the German Consulate can help you get out earlier. Go there and speak with them."

"Thank you. I was thinking about the same. I will figure it out. Hopefully, the Consulate has a plan, or they have already negotiated special deals with Lufthansa to get all German people out."

The Islamists had taken over the country. Despite the risk of being discovered as the enemy in their eyes, I decided to go to the Consulate anyway. I wanted to leave the country as soon as possible. Driving alone to the German Consulate was dangerous because it was located near the Bazaar in the south of Tehran, where the source of the revolution had started. I feared for my life because the people who lived there could not read or write. They would perceive every white-skinned, English-speaking man or woman as one of their enemies.

I would have been quickly spotted. With that in mind, they would not ask for my passport first, nor would I be able to explain myself. I was afraid to be tortured, shot, or stoned to death immediately. These were my options.

I took a cab from the northern part of the city down to the German Consulate. I wanted to get out of the country as early as I could. When

I arrived at the Consulate, I paid for the taxicab, got out, and rang the bell. No response or reply. All gates and doors were locked. Anxiously looking around the street to see whether somebody would watch me, I rang repeatedly. I was nervous and could hardly breathe. I knew I was in the right place because the agricultural representative invited me to a reception there a few weeks earlier. The employees of the German Consulate are supposed to stay in the building of the Consulate, being available for and to protect the citizens from Germany. Yet, it seemed the officers from the German Consulate had already left the sinking boat. They weren't there anymore. This place was empty. The official German Consulate had already evacuated their employees and sent them home. The German citizens were left alone in the war zone.

And AIESEC? I had been waiting to hear from anyone since day one of the revolution. I am still awaiting AIESEC's response regarding supporting me in leaving Iran or connecting with the German embassy. There was nothing but silence in the darkness. I couldn't leave earlier than planned initially. I had to wait four weeks to return to Germany using my booked flight. Thus, I needed to change my strategy for the next four weeks to survive.

With my head down, I walked to the street with traffic to catch another taxicab to the office and speak to my American boss.

"What should I do?"

"Well, first, you have to stop working because a woman in an Islamic state is not allowed to work. Second, the best way to survive is to be perceived as a local Iranian woman. Thus, you would become invisible to Islamists."

"Aha…what does that mean?"

It was a brilliant idea.

"Well, never show your city map again in public. That would be my easiest advice when you go from A to B. You don't want to be discovered as a Western tourist. Prepare where you are going before leaving the house and entering a street. You'll be fine. You already know the city very well."

"Okay, I can do that, no problem."

"You must adapt. That means wear the chador whenever you leave the house or our office. Learn the body language of Iranian women. It is more difficult than you think. Watch them and copy them. It will help you, although you will be almost covered with the chador. But you must walk and talk like them with their mannerisms, head and chin up, your shoulders straight, and you must walk slowly, not run. Watch the women and copy them."

"That's easier said than done. They are all covered up, so it's hard to see," I replied.

"Yes, but they are covered only in public, not at home. At home, they look as normal as everybody else. Wearing a chador or burqa is public protection for a woman. No other man in public should see a woman's body, hairline, or hair, nor in their regular, everyday clothes. You must cover up in public. The next time you will be invited to an Iranian dinner or lunch, watch the women. There will only be women, anyhow. Events with mixed men and women are no longer allowed or stated as politically correct.

"Lastly, always speak Farsi in public. Never speak English or German in public while you are in Iran. NEVER again."

I wore a black chador when I left the house. I carefully watched the women, how they walked and talked, and their mannerisms and gestures. Persian women keep their heads and chin up, shoulders and backs up in pride and straight. They don't walk like most women in the Western world, leaning forward and rushing to the next appointment. Persian women walk calmly and confidently, one step after the other. They don't run; they don't need to. I have never seen an Iranian woman in a hurry, putting her head and shoulders ahead of her feet, as seen by many busy European and American women, including myself. Instead, Iranian women embody confidence, self-esteem, grace, and dignity. I trained in copying and pasting as best as I could. My survival depended on it.

From day one in Tehran, I trained myself to catch and use a taxicab and had many chances to observe Iranian women. I learned the basics of their language, Farsi. I did not want anybody to discover me as a European or an American woman. I no longer spoke English in public; it took a lot of work, discipline, and focus. Often, I had to bite my tongue, and my inner guidance forced me to follow the Islamic rules. I would either talk in Farsi or shut my mouth.

I learned another vital survival rule every woman in any Islamic country knows. Never look directly into the eyes of a Muslim man you don't know. You must look down or aside when a man looks at you —a gesture of subservience and humility, a forced gesture for every woman. In doing so, it makes her seemingly invisible. This way, a woman doesn't attract any attention from men, which is a relief in times of violence. That's what I did, too. I didn't look into the eyes of any man who was a stranger to me, especially when he looked at me with curiosity or in awe. Even today, in our open-minded Western world, I don't look straight into the eyes of a man except in a business context. This survival tactic went into the depth of every cell of my body.

Mohsen stopped visiting us but called Bob occasionally to ensure we were okay. I missed him a lot. Before, we had seen each other almost every day, or at least we spoke on the phone. I missed our innocent, loving, happy life together, walking the parks, playing tennis, going into restaurants, or attending our favorite dinner dance. We had talked a lot, sharing our views of life and plans. We had a deep, meaningful connection. He was open-minded and appreciated people from the Western world. Thus, my perception and assessment of him had been entirely different and needed to be corrected. I had underestimated his deep faith as a Muslim and his strict following of the rules of the Koran.

Even with my training in body language and speaking Farsi, I was unsure whether suspicious and fanatic Islamists would discover my Western origins. I occasionally visited my former employer at the market research company because I couldn't stay home all day 24/7 for weeks doing nothing until my scheduled flight could bring me home. Every time, I had to drive downtown and get back home again. It felt like a raffle whether I would be discovered as the enemy or not, knowing what would happen if caught. My heart pounded against my chest whenever I went out in public, but I kept doing what I learned to do: wearing a fully covering chador and fluently speaking Farsi. I put up my arm, waved for a taxi, called my next stop, got in the car, looked down or out the window, watched people, cars, and armed forces pass, paid for the ride, and left the taxicab again. I merged into the secret world of Iranian women. Nobody seemed to care or get suspicious about me any longer.

Ellen and I had to buy food and groceries one day. We went together because she lived in Tehran for several years and spoke Farsi well. I wanted to learn more about how to behave in public. We drove downtown to our favorite marketplace. When we had gathered our fresh vegetables, fruits, and pistachios, we went to the cashier. The guy behind the booth was proud of his fresh products. Ellen started chatting with him, appreciating his great selection of vegetables. I didn't say anything, looked around, and held my breath.

Then, the man looked at me and asked in Farsi, "Are you an Armenian woman, too?"

I was surprised because I wasn't involved in the chat. "Are you asking me?"

"Yes, I am asking you."

His voice had a threatening undertone. Ellen looked at me with her big, blue eyes, slightly frightened, but didn't say a word so as not to make him suspicious.

Fortunately, I understood his question.

"Baleh," which means, "Yes, I am," while shaking my head. I did not look him in his eyes but shied away and down to the floor. Ellen paid for the groceries, and we walked out with heads up, shoulders straight, as calm as possible.

"Why did he ask me that question?" I asked Ellen later at home.

"I don't know, but people from Armenia are mixed races between Europeans and people from Arabic countries. He wanted to ensure we were one of them and not the enemy. I have seen several with blue eyes and sometimes even lighter hair. Iranian women's hair is usually dark blue-black. Every time I asked them, they were from Armenia."

"Ah, that's why. I am glad that I instinctively confirmed without knowing."

Sometimes during the night, I would be awakened by the insistent screaming of women and the sound of shootings. These sounds are unbearable.

I often went to the living room to find Bob sitting at the bar, drinking his glass of whiskey. He couldn't endure it either. I would join him with a glass of wine, and we would talk all night about the meaning of life and what was happening around us. Neither of us could go back to sleep. He liked me, and I wanted him as a friend. I never told him what I knew about his wife. He might have known. I was glad that he never asked me.

We heard couples in the neighborhood yelling at each other while standing on the street. They were fighting about something. During the Civil War, those fights ended in the same sad way every time: a shot and the screaming stopped—another woman killed by her husband or a relative right around the corner. We remained silent, sitting at the bar. Neither one of us went out to see what was happening. It would have been suicide. Laws were not abided by anymore. Self-justice had become the new law, another tragic reality in civil wars. Rules change, and the life of a human being has no meaning anymore.

People only behave according to rules in front of the military patrol. Obedience and submission are the highest duties. You only do what they command you to do. Military controls had become part of my daily routine as well. I remembered my father's advice, who had worked many years in Argentina during Juan Peron's regime. Daily, on his way to the construction site, the company he worked for changed his direction, the car, the driver, and military checks. It had become part of his professional life.

"So what will you do when asked for the passport?" Dad had asked me before I left for Tehran, giving me the answer immediately.

"Certainly, do not reach into your jacket, purse, or the car's glove compartment to take them out."

"Why not?" I asked innocently. I had no clue.

"Military or police patrol will think you will grab a gun hidden in your purse or the car compartment. They expect the worst. They will kill you first and fast because they will feel threatened."

"Okay, so what should I do instead?"

"Always put your hands on the steering wheel so they can see them. Refrain from putting your hand in your pockets, purse, or elsewhere. Always be highly alert and careful and assume the worst.

Don't ask any questions; don't start discussing, arguing, or defending yourself. Keep your mouth shut. They also do not want to know if you just came from buying groceries. They are trained not to get emotionally involved, distracted, or sympathetic to you. They assume that you are a threat and thus will shoot first. They don't believe you have good intentions. If you dig in your purse, they will kill you in the blink of an eye. They will kill you before you even have a chance to say something. Human lives, foremost women's lives, don't have any significance in war times, and certainly not in any Islamic country.

The best survival strategy is to simply tell them where your passport is while you keep your hands up. Then, let them take your passport out themselves. You don't do anything but wait; don't move, and don't say anything. You are an enemy no matter who will ask you, man or woman. Only a dead man or woman is a good man or woman in war zones."

I thought about my dad often. He must have experienced and watched a lot of violence in his professional career, working in almost every country all over the world.

*   *   *

A few Europeans who had met at several Consulate events discussed the latest news in Tehran, what to do about it, and the best or most straightforward way to leave the country. We usually gathered at a friend's house in the afternoon and left around 7:00 p.m. The guys had cars, so they drove the others home who didn't. I remember sitting in one of these houses in a simple furnished living room and kitchen; window shades had to be down even during the day, and no lights turned on. We didn't want to call the attention of suspicious neighbors. We lit candles. We were talking quietly and whispering. The chances that the neighbors would call the military were high, and we anxiously sat together on high alert.

On one of these evenings, when one guy brought me home, we got stopped by a military patrol, although it was early. We had to step out of the car. One soldier turned his machine gun on us. We had presented our passports to the other officer, who asked for them. I wore my chador, kept my head and eyes down, and said nothing. Fortunately, the driver spoke Farsi fluently and answered all their questions. After a seeming eternity being looked at suspiciously, we could continue.

On another evening, we were late departing the weekly gathering. We knew we had to drive another forty-five minutes to get home. One German guy recklessly drove the car to match the 8:00 p.m. curfew hour. We knew we couldn't do it, even though he was going as fast as he could. Between 8:00 p.m. and 8:30 p.m., before I arrived at Bob and Ellen's house, I had mentally died several deaths. He observed the streets to the left, and I had to watch the roads on the right side to tell him when I saw military patrol so that he would slow down. I prayed to God that there should be no military or police waiting, approaching to kill us. Other than being seen on the street during curfew hours, they would have had a right to do so without reason. It was nerve-wracking, but we were lucky.

For the remaining weeks in Tehran, day and night, I was on high alert observing my environment.

*   *   *

Even being on high alert doesn't protect you from bombs hidden under a chair in a restaurant. I was lucky when, ten minutes after I left the restaurant, a bomb exploded and killed everyone still sitting there. I remember that feeling clearly when I heard the news an hour later.

After a while, I started to calm down and felt less anxious. This is the survival mode in each of us that activates when we can neither fight nor escape. We freeze. I got used to the terror around me, realizing that the human body and heart can only endure emotional pain for a limited time.

I became acclimated. I had fewer panic attacks and less anxiety. Seeing one dead person on the street or several is horrible, but after a while, you get used to it. This sounds shocking and brutal. War is shocking and cruel.

My frozen, numb state of mind and heart was the best way to deal with everything. My innate wisdom told me not to think at all. I shut off and lived day by day, managing only what was coming up next. I switched from panic mode into alert calmness, keeping my emotions, and often my shaking hands, under control.

I trusted my intuition and God's protection. I didn't want to feed my thoughts into any emotional reaction. I tried to make the right decision and act accordingly.

I commanded myself daily: stop thinking about it, with no pity for myself or empathy for anybody else. I thought of my life as an emergency doctor who must deal with heavily injured people. They cannot help someone when they feel sorry or shocked about what they see. Intuitively, I knew that my chances of survival would be good if I could pull myself together and control my emotions.

Four weeks after Black Friday, I finally left and returned to Germany, leaving Bob, Ellen, and Mohsen behind. Mohsen picked me up at the house where I had found a lovely and loving home for three months. I was very sad the day I left. I had fallen in love with this country and my Iranian friend. I had to say goodbye to Bob and Ellen, my new friends and protectors.

"It's the best you can do. I will follow up with you in a couple of months. We will meet in Germany," Ellen promised.

My heart was heavy. Everybody knew it was wishful thinking because staying in Tehran meant any day, someone could kill her and the entire family. But hope dies last.

"We will be going back by the end of the year, but Bob has to stay till February because of his job."

"Let's stay in touch, and let me know when you will be arriving, too. I will pick you up at the airport this time," I said, smiling and remembering the first day we met at the airport in Tehran. Although it had only been three months, it seemed years had passed.

"I will write you."

"Not every letter will arrive, but we can ask friends or colleagues who will go to Germany to take the letter and send it to you. And the other way around. You can give them your letter so we can stay in contact and figure out when we will meet."

"Sounds great. Let's do that."

Mohsen grabbed my suitcase, put it in the car, and opened the door for me the last time. No one said a word. I opened my window, and while he started the engine, I waved with both hands to Ellen and Bob and sent air kisses.

Neither Mohsen nor I said a word. Arriving at the airport, he parked the car, picked up my luggage, and walked me to the check-in counter. I looked around the building, remembering the day I arrived in Tehran.

"I can't believe that it was only three months ago that I arrived here. It feels like three years; so many things have happened. Here, I met Bob and Ellen for the first time."

"I was lost, not knowing where to go and what to do, thinking about flying back home the next day. I could never have imagined what would happen during the following months. I am grateful that I stayed and met all of you who have become dear friends and changed my life—in good times and bad times."

"Great that you changed your mind and stayed."
Mohsen replied, smiling.

He was standing in line with me, waiting for the check-in. He was a genuine gentleman with whom I fell in love the minute we met. During my entire time in Tehran, I felt he had put a shield over me and had protected us in the background. I was scared but didn't feel lost or devastated during the revolution. I knew at heart somehow I would leave safely.

When we arrived at the check-in counter, Mohsen put my luggage on the baggage claim.

"You must take care of yourself from now on."

He had tears in his eyes. I could feel the pain inside his heart. We knew we wouldn't see each other again, not in this lifetime.

"I hope that you will have a safe flight. You will have a great time coming home to your family and friends. They will surely be happy to see you again. However, Tehran has become your second home. You may come back one day. Let me know for sure. I will miss you."

"Tehran has become the home of my heart because of you, Mohsen."

I tried cheering him up and touched his arm. I was sad, too.

"Without you, I would not have considered staying and getting my MBA at the Iranian Management School. You showed me your world, which is lovely, gorgeous, heartfelt, and unique. I will always remember Tehran as it was when we first met three months ago. I will never forget the country, the desert, the cities, and the Caspian Sea, and I will never forget you, Mohsen. I miss you already, too. I can't thank you enough from the bottom of my heart for everything you have done for me."

I looked into his gorgeous black eyes and long black eyelashes. I wanted to hug him, but that was against the rules. We couldn't hug each other in public, nor could our hands touch. I felt heavy with tons of rocks in my heart.

We slowly walked to the passport control. Mohsen stopped, and I had to show my passport to the officers. I turned around one last time. Mohsen was still standing there, frozen. Stony-faced, he was gazing at me. I could feel his sadness and pain as much as mine. It was heartbreaking for me to see him also heartbroken.

I waved and then put my hand up to cover my mouth and looked down, not to show him that I started to cry.

I was too naïve and couldn't understand, but he knew from the beginning that we would never have a future together. His conservative family would never have allowed that to happen. For the first time, it occurred to me so clearly that it's not simply the faith we are raised in and practicing. What divides us humans are the rules and regulations of our religion and society, forcing us to live by them. We are prisoners of our culture, the world created and taught by the people around us, and the incidents happening in our lifetime. No escape is possible, even if we believe we have free will and are free. We are not. Everyone lives in their bubble.

I walked through passport and security control, boarded the plane, found my seat, and removed my chador. I wouldn't need it anymore back in Germany. I sighed. A strong feeling of relief and security made room for breathing and sighs, letting go of the permanent anxiety and fear of the last four weeks. I was blessed to have survived.

When the flight attendant offered me a glass of water, I nodded and started crying. "Water is the most precious source of the world." I heard

Mohsen saying. Almost the entire flight back to Germany, I was sobbing. I was letting go of the trauma of all that had happened to me in the last three months. I began my trip by getting arrested in Moscow on my way to Tehran to find myself trapped in a civil war where religious cultures and lifestyles clashed in every sense. I was grateful to have survived these traumatic experiences.

I also painfully realized that I had to leave my dearest friends and the man I loved.

A few days after returning home to Cologne, Germany, I met my student colleagues in our favorite bar to celebrate my homecoming.

My appearance must have changed a lot because some didn't immediately recognize me. One of my fellow students looked at me with a mixture of amazement and admiration, shaking his head:

"You have grown up in the last three months."

"Yep" ….I nodded my head.

Two years after I returned from Tehran, I finished my studies. I graduated with a master's in business administration and started a career in management.

Story 2: Truth & Consequences

1 9 8 5

Jim was about my height, had dark hair and green eyes, and was handsome, charming, and an ambitious man who seemed quite successful in his career.

My due diligence ended there, at this superficial level. For him, I gave up my job and moved from a city in the South to one in the Far North.

Did I ever think about what kind of a man I would want and need by my side? Nope. I had turned twenty-eight and was anxious to find a decent husband. Being unmarried would have been a shame to the family in the mid-twentieth century. That's what my mother taught me, day in and day out since I had turned sixteen. Although I had finished high school, studied at a university, and gotten a master's degree in business administration, marriage was still more for a young woman back then. Like a little voice, I often heard my mother speaking to me about finding a husband as soon as possible and before I turned thirty. I knew the basis of a marriage needed to be more stable than just fulfilling a demand of my mother, but I didn't want to search forever.

My inner voice and heart had already spoken to me on our wedding day. When I heard the minister asking Jim the most essential question, "Will you….?" I was shocked, and my mind cleared in an instant.

I realized what I was about to do. My thoughts were swirling.

OMG, what am I doing here? No, I can't marry that man. This is a big mistake. How did this happen? I shouldn't do this.

I turned around and looked at my father, stepmom, sister, and future mother-in-law, the witnesses. They were so excited and seemed so happy, beaming at me.

I can't do that to them. I can't call off the wedding now.

I was thinking, shaking my head. Jim looked at me, frightened. He knew me and realized what I was going through.

"Will you, Gabby, marry Jim . . ."

The minister looked at me. It was my turn now.

"Yes, I will."

Jim grinned joyfully, putting the golden ring on my finger. I could have ended the wedding with a lot of turmoil and drama but without significant scars on my heart. Jim would have been devastated, which I didn't want to happen. I was the good girl who didn't make anyone feel bad or hurt.

I often think my father would have understood my saying no at the last minute and in front of everyone. My dad would have laughed and asked me to pay back his investment. Ultimately, I paid much more for not having had the guts to say no.

After our wedding, Jim and I moved into one of the well-established areas of the city. White Victorian-style villas from the nineteenth century, framed with black iron railings and fences, and beautiful flowers in well-kept gardens are adequate for the old chestnut trees in the streets, giving the district a typical character. This wealthy residential area was very green due to its many parks and was close to the waterfront of a colossal river. The river has been the pathway for container ships arriving worldwide for centuries. The port has made the city and its people wealthy and famous as shipowners.

We lived in a one-bedroom apartment under the roof of one of these old villas. Shortly after I had moved and found a new job, Jim signed up for a unique job opportunity five hundred miles away in another city in the South. Thus, living together in our tiny apartment was easy because we met only during the weekend. We lived close to the big river; from there, we could hear the foghorns of these massive container ships coming in at night. Especially in wintertime, it was spooky because of the thick fog. You could barely see anything beyond thirty feet.

Right around the corner, my two best friends, Jack and Angela, also lived in one of the Victorian-style villas. We had become neighbors accidentally. It happened just like that. I had known Jack since our time together at the university, where we both studied and finished business administration and economics with master's degrees. Over time, we became friends and stayed in touch.

Jack met Angela during a friend's party. She was a very confident and self-assured woman who worked in finance. She had her own rules for everything and everyone and always seemed to have the correct answer to every question, sometimes without being asked. She told us how life should work for her, Jack, and the rest of us, including me. Nonetheless, I liked her a lot. Jack loved and married her because she gave him the stability he had always wanted in a relationship. Angela was honest, proverbially carrying her heart on her sleeve. Even without being asked, she would always tell you what she thought, felt, liked, and disliked, and for sure, what you should consider, feel, like, and how to treat or react to people. Her self-esteem and communication were assertive and impressive. No one dared to contradict her.

I liked walking to the office from our apartment. The manufacturing company was a short ten-minute walk away from my home. I loved my new job in marketing management with one of the most renowned family-owned companies in Germany. The company, a multinational, billion-dollar enterprise, was founded and successfully built up by two brothers from scratch. These two brothers became wealthy and well-respected members of the high society. The two-story office building sits right in the middle of a park. I learned that the mansion was the family's former home, which had been turned into our offices when the company was sold to a private investor. Approximately a hundred and fifty people worked there. Next to the building were two smaller ones. One bungalow had been converted from a huge swimming pool /wellness area into a canteen for all employees.

The other bungalow accommodated a grand entrance hall and a library in a gallery you would look up to when entering the entrance hall. Two staterooms served as offices for the two brothers, a smaller library with a fireplace for fireside chats, a vast conference room seating at least twenty people on one conference table, and a considerable living hall with two fireplaces on each side facing the park. These were the representative buildings for meetings and events with famous and influential people. Previously, the two colossal conference rooms had been the family's living room and dining room. I was impressed because it was pure luxury compared to the world I came from, which wasn't poor at all. How did people live in these multidimensional sizes?

I remember an impressive, tall wooden statue of a carved-out and painted Native American man standing between the conference room and living hall. On the bottom of the wood block where the Native American was standing, my maiden name was engraved. I was stunned, and I felt awkward at the same time. Nobody could tell me the story of this Native American statue with my name carved in it. Still, everyone was as surprised as me seeing this guy every time we walked into the conference room. At that point in time, I had no connection to the Native American culture and history. That would profoundly change several years later.

I felt privileged to work in the most beautiful workplace I could have imagined. I also had great colleagues who supported me as the new kid on the block.

When I entered the building one morning, I ran into my former boss, Josh. He was always in a good mood. I had never seen him grumpy. Josh made me smile instantly. I liked him a lot because he joked and had funny stories to entertain everyone. Josh was one of the guys who always lived on the bright side of life.

I walked into my office, which I had to myself. It was tiny, with a desk and a chair, but with a huge floor-to-ceiling window and a glass door with direct access to a balcony. Most importantly, I had a great view of the park all day and could watch the four seasons pass. My current boss, Liam, had his office beside me. This day, he was already meeting with colleagues to discuss the best marketing strategy for a new product launch.

I sat down and screened the papers I had worked on the week before. Liam had asked me to draft a presentation for a new promotion program for the latest advertising launch. I had already started working on it a week ago, but today was the day I had to present my ideas to him. I had some great ideas, but simply telling them was never enough because of how much money was involved. I had to sell him my thoughts using a logical and analytical approach, talking about the target groups, the whys, and possible results, considering objectives, the execution plan, and the given budget. I was in a hurry and had only three hours to draft an excellent presentation. He wanted me to meet in the afternoon, right after lunch.

I closed the doors of my office and started right off. I was in my flow and liked what I was doing. Nobody disturbed me; not even Liam knocked on the door when he returned from his meeting. He knew that when my doors were closed, it meant, "Do not disturb, please." And he didn't.

The phone rang when I returned from my short lunch break and walked into the office. My gynecologist, Dr. Miller, was on the other line. I was surprised that he called me directly.

"So, what's up?" I asked him.

He started to speak, but I could hardly hear him.

"I can't understand you. Please speak a little louder."

He cleared his throat and started again, his voice stumbling. "Gabby, what I am about to tell you is quite challenging. We did the blood test and discovered that your hormone results are all out of sorts. I have never seen those numbers before. I don't know what to do with them."

What did he say? He kept talking for about five minutes. I could hear what he said, but these words didn't reach my brain.

"I assume that you have a cancerous tumor somewhere in your body... and that it is a highly aggressive one because it has created a level of testosterone in your body that is multiple times higher than every man has ever had!"

I woke up from my far-away mindset.

"What did you just say? I have cancer? Now what? What do you want me to do?"

I didn't understand what he was saying or what that could mean for me. I was still hopeful that he would help me regain my health.

"I am not sure, but if it is the malignancy I would expect, looking at your numbers, you'll have only six months to live. You have to go into a hospital instantly. There will be experts who will check your body, searching for the cause."

"Which hospital should I go to? Do you have a recommendation?" I replied with an equally stumbling voice, hoping he would advise me.

"I don't know. You can go to any hospital, but you need to find out where you can find the experts in your case. I can't help you with that. I am sorry, Gabby. Goodbye."

Then, he hung up, leaving me in shock. I stared in disbelief at the phone. What? What had just happened?

I didn't understand and couldn't feel anything. It was like walking through a thick fog in a forest, where all the sounds were muffled.

Dread overcame me as I looked out of the window. Everything seemed normal, as if nothing had happened. How could this be? Birds were singing, and people were walking along the sidewalk. The doctor's message seemed so far away.

Maybe I misunderstood him?

Usually, I could hear my colleagues speaking in the other offices or on the floor. But at that moment, their voices came from far away. Or maybe they had listened to everything, and now they were whispering? I felt weird. I felt like I was sitting in a room with walls made of glass. I could look outside and see them moving their mouths while talking, but I couldn't hear what they said.

Only six months to live? That was short. I was thinking and started counting the months with my fingers. It was the beginning of June. Could I celebrate Christmas if I was lucky? That would be okay—at least one Christmas together. I love Christmas. I could not think further or into the New Year.

I had no idea what to do, what to say, or whom to call for advice. I was frozen in shock as I entered my boss's office to give my presentation. I took a chair, sat at his desk, and placed the charts before him. I explained the objectives and target groups to walk him through the presentation. In between, he looked at me with a worried expression.

"Is there something wrong? Did I miss an important part?" Now, I was worried.

"What happened to you?"

"Nothing. Why do you ask?"

"Well, your skin is as gray as these walls. Don't tell me that nothing is going on. I know you a little bit. Two hours earlier, you looked much healthier and happier than now. Do you want to speak about what happened?"

I felt embarrassed. I never wanted to speak about my most private things and never did to anyone. But Liam insisted, and he was very concerned.

"Do you feel well? Shall I call a doctor?"

"Do I look so terrible?"

"You do look quite unhealthy. I am worried."

He looked me deep into my eyes. I had to look away.

"What is going on?"

"Well, I don't know what to say. Half an hour ago, my gynecologist called me strangely. Do you want to go into the details and find out what he was telling me?"

"Yes, indeed. I am the father of twin girls. There is always something going on!"

"My doctor told me he thinks I have a malignancy somewhere in my body. He also told me that if a third party confirmed his cancer diagnosis, I would only have six months to live. And that he has no idea who could help me any further."

"What..?" Liam took a deep breath. He was shocked.

"I don't know what to do right now. I am lost and devastated, and I can't think. It's hard to describe how I feel right now."

"What else did your doctor say or recommend?"

"Nothing. The doctor said he could no longer help me because he was not an expert in dealing with this. I should go into a hospital to find out what is happening."

"That's it? No recommendation on which hospital you could go to? Or the name of an expert here or in another city? He should know. I can't believe it!"

Liam's face turned red. He was indignant over the doctor's reaction, leaving me with a cancer diagnosis and no further assistance or recommendations.

I was indifferent, in a kind of paralysis, with no tears, despair, anxiety, or fear. No, nothing but numbness internally. Shock.

"So what would you do if you were in my shoes? I don't know any experts or a hospital that could check and treat me properly here in the city or elsewhere."

"I know someone. He is a medical doctor and a friend of mine. I will immediately call him and ask him what you should do."

He picked up the phone and talked to the head of the cancer department in one major hospital in the city, which is well known for its cancer treatment.

"Listen, I have an emergency case here. In front of me sits my junior manager. She just got bad news: a cancer diagnosis without any proof and a forecasted six-month lifespan. It's a horrible message based on an assumption. We are all shocked."

He nodded and listened to the man on the other end of the phone.

"Great. Thank you. Appreciate it."

He hung up.

"What did he say?" I asked anxiously.

"Next week, you will check in at the hospital, and they will investigate what is the source of this horrible diagnosis. They might confirm it or find something else about what is happening to you."

I was grateful to have such a boss like Liam. He had arranged that I would have a bed and a full medical check at the hospital's cancer department a week later.

He took care of me, and I felt relieved. Something would likely happen, but I don't know what it would be. I might only have six more months to live; perhaps something else would happen. I was confused and anxious and silently hoped that things would turn out for the better.

Liam told everybody in the company what had happened. I felt embarrassed to answer all their questions and tell my story again. I didn't want to stand in the center of everybody's attention. However, I felt comforted that people cared about me. My colleagues showered me with support and the feeling that they would stay with me till the end. At least I would not be alone, whatever happened during this time. Their caring attitude helped me not think about possible consequences so soon.

Thoughts of sadness and grief crawled up at night when I was alone. I had difficulty sleeping and often woke up in the middle of the night. I wondered if I'd survive surgery because my aunt Mary died during surgery on her thyroid when the doctors discovered cancer there.

When Jim came home the following weekend, I told him what happened.
"Let's see what the hospital exams will tell you. It would help if you don't worry beforehand."

" What? I am scared to death."

He shrugged his shoulders and turned on the TV.

"Wait and see. You can't do anything about it now."

I was disappointed and felt abandoned. He didn't show concern or emotion like my boss had the other day. Did he want to be cool?

*   *   *

The evening before I checked into the hospital, Liam invited my colleagues and me for dinner. Josh, Barbara, and Brigitte, with whom I already had become friends, were happy to join us. He took us to one of the best restaurants in town, followed by visiting a bar dance club. It was awesome. I had a lot of fun, and we partied all night until early in the morning. I wanted to stay awake and enjoy every minute before I had to check in at the hospital. It could be the last time I saw them. So, we drank and danced all night. I did not sleep for one minute. At 5:00 a.m., they called a taxi to drive me home; I asked the driver to wait, grabbed my luggage, and was driven to the hospital.

I checked into the hospital at 7:00 a.m., got into my room, put on my nightgown, and crawled into the bed. I was planning for the surgery the next day. The hospital nurse said hello and took a blood sample from my veins to define the potentiated narcosis. I fell asleep, missing breakfast and lunch.

"You must have partied a lot last night," the anesthesiologist commented when he and the surgeon visited me later that afternoon.

"Yes, and I am tired, but that's okay."

"I can imagine," answered the anesthetist with a smile.

"We have found some blood in your veins. There is more alcohol than blood in there." Both laughed.

"Okay…" I felt embarrassed.

"We will recheck your blood tonight, and when everything is okay, we can do the surgery tomorrow. We want to ensure your body is ready for that intervention."

It seemed all okay that evening. The following day, I got an injection to calm down. They gave me the anesthetic, and I was gone.

I looked into Angela and Jack's eyes first when I woke up. Both were sitting on my bed, waiting for me to wake up. How did they know? Their affection and care touched me. They were concerned about my health, and I was grateful to look into the eyes of my closest friends.

"Where is Jim?" Angela asked me.

"I don't know. I hoped Jim would arrive today instead of tomorrow. Maybe his boss didn't allow him to take a day or two off."

"I would quit that job if my boss tried to prevent me from seeing my wife in the hospital!" Jack shouted.

"Did he try to call and leave a message for you, or did he send some flowers with a message?" Angela offered.

"No, nothing yet."

Jack, my long-term friend from our Alma Mater, was upset. I was sad not to have gotten any messages from my husband, but I was too exhausted to get angry.

We shared a few words and a hug, and I fell asleep. I was still coming out from under anesthesia. A few hours later, I woke up again, and Barbara, one of my colleagues, was sitting on my bed. She took my hand and tried to comfort me. I fell asleep again. Another couple of hours later, I woke up, and Liam and Josh were sitting next to my bed. I couldn't believe it.

Almost everyone came to visit me. I was surprised and in awe. I knew I looked terrible. They didn't care but made jokes to make me laugh. I realized that each one of my closest friends and colleagues had a compassionate heart. They intuitively knew what counted under those circumstances.

No one from my family checked on me. My dad lived and worked in Portugal then, and my sister lived in another city about 250 miles south. They had delegated taking care of me to my husband.

Jim still hadn't arrived at my bed or called, and I wondered what was happening. Again, I felt abandoned.

The following day was Friday when my surgeon checked the saline drip and asked how I was doing.

"I am okay...the scar on my belly hurts, but I feel okay. So, what did you find out?" I asked anxiously.

"We didn't find a cancerous tumor, so this is the good news," he started. "The bad news: we could not find the reason for your extreme hormone numbers. We want to check your head as well. Maybe a tumor in your brain is the cause."

"What? A tumor in my brain? No way. Nobody in my family has ever had a tumor in the brain. How will you remove it? If you don't do it right, I might stop being able to think and act properly then. That's even worse."

"We will make an appointment for a computer tomography next week. Then we will talk again. You can go home for the weekend but must check in again Sunday afternoon."

He left. Was that, again, good news or bad news? The new shocking information was, again, based on an assumption.

I was sitting in my bed with my tumbling thoughts. What should I do?
I tried to figure out what to do next. I had yet to hear from Jim, so I decided to stay and wait. I did not want to go home alone because living under the roof of an ancient house without an elevator meant climbing all the stairs with an open cut in my belly.

Jim finally showed up early in the evening. I was grateful and relieved to see him and to go home. He would help me climb the stairs. I did not ask why he could not come earlier. I was relieved that he was there, that I wasn't alone during the weekend.

"Honey, I can go home for the weekend. I will tell you everything on our way. I'll let the nurse know to take away the saline drip, and then I will get dressed. You grab my stuff, and then off we go."

I smiled from one ear to the other. I was thrilled to return home finally, and I would worry about my brain next week.

"Sorry, honey, but that's impossible tonight," Jim replied. "I have already made a dinner appointment with my groomsman and his girlfriend. They are waiting in the lobby downstairs. I have only ten minutes. I will pick you up tomorrow morning. Then, we will talk about everything."

"What? No, no. Please. You could tell your friends you want to take me home now because I want to go home. They can go for dinner alone. I am sure they will understand."

"Listen, I had a tough week. Could you please not make a big deal out of it? Go to bed and get the rest you need. We will meet tomorrow morning. We will have the entire weekend to talk."

"Are you sure?"

"Yes, no worries. You can walk me to the elevator if you want."

I slowly walked him to the elevator while carrying my saline drip. I felt his impatience. He wanted to leave the hospital as soon as possible.

"Please go slower. I can't catch up with your speed. Are you sure you want to go now? It would make me happy if you would stay with me and take me home tonight."

The first time after those weeks of not knowing what to feel, my emotions came back. I became despondent. When we arrived at the elevator, I asked Jim again.

"Are you sure? I beg you, please don't leave me alone now."

"Don't worry. All is well. Have a good night. I will pick you up tomorrow morning," he said. He kissed my cheek and stepped into the elevator.

The shining silver door of the elevator closed, and I saw myself carrying the saline drip in the reflection of the doors, standing there in my nightgown. I looked at myself, and suddenly, I felt deeply lost.

I started crying, grabbed my saline drip, turned around, and slowly walked back to my room. I was exhausted and crashed. I crawled into my bed and cried for hours till I fell asleep.

The following day, I woke up with no more sadness or grief in my heart. I had no feelings at all. It was like an inner switch had turned off every emotion for my husband. I was done with him and the idea of a shared future. I was ready to look forward to a new life by myself, wherever and with whatever I would have to fight. I had to do it alone. Why should I be married to someone who wouldn't stand by me during my darkest hours and days? Why should I let him tell me what to do or not to do any longer? Why should I plan a future with him if he cared more about himself than his wife? He, who was supposed to be the father of my future children? I had lost my trust.

Jim picked me up late in the morning, drove home, and we spent a quiet weekend watching TV and ordering pizza. We only talked a little. He did not ask me any questions about what happened, but he did ask me to do his laundry in the basement.

"Do you not care what's happening to me? Why don't you ask what the doctors had done, why I had to spend a week in a hospital? Aren't you interested in what they said about my surgery, the diagnosis, and the next steps? I am shocked. I will tell you something: you get your damn dirty laundry cleaned by yourself. I am not your housekeeper."

That was the end of the conversation for the entire weekend. Sunday afternoon, I took a taxi to the hospital, and Jim took the next flight to return to work in the South. We hadn't spoken a word since I had yelled at him with my truth.

Monday morning, I called Richard, a friend of mine who was a marketing executive in Munich. He had already asked me years before to join his marketing team, but I had always rejected the offer. I was afraid I was not good enough for the job and his team because he had such a brilliant and bright mind. But now, I wasn't anxious anymore. I was ready to start a new life and job in a new city.

On the phone, I told him what had happened. Richard was surprised to hear.

"Are you going to come to Munich, finally?" he asked me, laughing.

"Yes, I would love to if you have a job for me."

"Seriously? Let's talk for real. I will catch a flight and visit you in the hospital tomorrow."

That was an instant reaction. I would have expected this from my husband, but not merely from a colleague.

The next afternoon, Richard arrived. We walked up and down the hospital corridor while talking. I told him everything about what had happened, including the story of my husband.

"I am ready to get a divorce, leave the city, and find a new job in Munich."

"I am glad to hear that. Your husband isn't the right match for you. You know that I don't like him. You are much smarter than him. It's about time you come to Munich. You will like it. I have an open position if you live longer than six months," he laughed. He was serious.

"Really?"

"Yes, I have always wanted you on my team. I want to hire you tomorrow, but you must convince my company peers, too. That's the rule. Call me when you leave the hospital, and we will arrange an all-day interview with my team. You will meet my peers and my boss. You should be okay, but they have to approve as well. And I will cross my fingers regarding the brain thing."

"That works for me," I replied happily. A new future dawned on the horizon.

The next night at the hospital, I woke up at 4:00 a.m. I couldn't sleep any longer. I thought about everything I would have to do, the people I needed to talk to, and my relocation to Munich. I hadn't told my husband and friends about my intentions yet because I wanted to close the deal with the new job first.

I was sure none of my friends or colleagues would understand my decision, but I had to do it. I wanted to leave everything behind me and start fresh with a new, positive outlook on my future, a new life from scratch. I was sure I wouldn't lose my real friends.

I stood up in the middle of the night, put on my bathrobe, and walked along the corridor. It was dark, and there was only a dim light in the room where the night nurse was sitting. A big window to the park opened at the end of the corridor. Two chairs were there. I took one of them, looking out to the city lights. A few minutes later, an elderly lady approached me.

"May I sit here, too?" she asked. "I can't sleep."

"Yes, please. I can't sleep either."

She sat down, and neither of us said anything for a while. We both looked out the window.

"What is your name?" she asked me suddenly.

"Gabby".

"And what are you doing here?"

I told her my story.

"And what are you doing for work?" she asked again. She seemed a curious old lady who loved to hear stories.

"I work for a great company a little outside of downtown. I have great colleagues, and it's the best place I could have imagined to work. The offices, canteen, and conference room are amazing. Everything is beautiful. My office sits in a huge park where I walk daily after lunch with my colleagues. I think it's the most gorgeous workplace in Germany."

"That sounds great. It's been a long time since I was in this area," she replied and smiled.

"So, what is your name, and what brought you here?" I asked her. I didn't want to be disrespectful.

"I am the widow of one of the men who founded the company you are working for."

"What! No way."

I was stunned. I couldn't believe the woman sitting next to me called her former home and living room where we had meetings all day. She had swum in the pool, which had become my canteen. What a coincidence. I shook my head in awe.

"I lived there for decades till my husband died, and my brother-in-law sold the company to a private investor, a famous family and entrepreneurs, too."

That night, till the sun rose, she told me the incredible story of her life and her family who had lived right there where I worked. She spoke about all the details, how the swimming pool looked before it became a canteen, the vast living room that became our conference room, and the Native American sculpture standing there. She told me it was a wedding gift, but she couldn't remember why my maiden name was carved at the bottom of the sculpture. As the wife of one company owner, she had created the interior design and led the architects and designers to build her husband's and her family's homes. It was her signature in the conference room, the library, and the fireside chat room. She told me all the stories about the events and famous people she hosted there. Her life was spectacular until her husband died. Then, she got into fights with their only son. Finally, he stopped talking to her. She hasn't met her grandson yet and has lived a lonesome life since then. Only her chauffeur accompanied her every day.

"I am not allowed to see my grandson, which makes me sad," she finished with a sad tone.

I felt so sorry for her. It was sad listening to the story of her rich and famous life. Ultimately, she was abandoned, although she had raised her son and done many good things for others. We both were women who were left alone unexpectedly. It made me even more secure in striving for a new beginning in another city. Sometimes, having the proper distance, even measured in miles, is the best cure for a heartbroken soul.

*   *   *

"There is a spot the size of a pea right in front of your brain, where the hypothalamus sits," the medical assistant said after analyzing the X-ray of my brain CT a week later.

"See, have a look yourself."

"Okay, but I can't see anything. I am not an expert here. I believe you. What will happen next? Are they going to open my skull?" I asked with wide eyes. I already felt the hammer knocking on my head and opening my skullcap.

"You don't need to be scared of facing brain surgery. It is not that difficult. The doctor can remove this little tumor while leading the scalpel through your nose. They won't open or break up your skull. Don't worry."

I was concerned.

"A scalpel through my nose? What if they accidentally cut off some of my brain because they shake their hands or sneeze suddenly?"

"I will present the results to your MD and the other experts from the brain surgery department. They will let you know what the next steps will be."

I gasped for breath.

"And when will they let me know about their decision and next steps?"

"It will take a while. It is the end of July, and several MDs are vacationing. So, don't expect further instructions before the next four weeks, probably the end of August. Till then, nothing dangerous or life-threatening will happen. You can leave the hospital tomorrow, and we will get back to you when we have more news."

I sighed, still uncertain of what would happen. I returned to my room, packed my stuff, signed off, hailed a cab, and went home. Should I be happy? What would a brain tumor or surgery mean? What would come next?

At the end of July, I flew to Munich for an all-day interview for the new job. It was a tough day of investigative questions about my skills and competencies. Finally, I got the approval from all managers and executives who interviewed me. I hadn't told my husband yet what I was planning. I wanted to wait until I was finally sure I would be healthy again and then make a move. I still felt deeply shaken and traumatized about what had happened and remained hurt by his unempathetic behavior. I no longer wanted this man by my side.

A few days after my birthday, at the beginning of September, the hospital called me. The assistant asked to schedule an appointment to meet the professor, the chief medical doctor of the hospital. He was not only the head of the clinic but also a professor at a medical school.

"The professor? Oh my god, the head of the clinic. This is going to be a challenging talk." I expected the worst.

When I entered his office, he offered me a chair at a round meeting table and sat beside me.

"We could not figure out the reasons for your fatal hormone numbers, but you don't have cancer or a brain tumor."

"But one of your assistants saw a spot in front of my head. What makes you sure there is no tumor in my body?"

"It was a false diagnosis from the assistant," he replied.

"What? Again? A false diagnosis? But why did you leave me in the dark, anxious, and uncertain for over four weeks?"

"We knew that you would be okay, but you are right. We should not have let you wait so long."

I told him the entire story, beginning with the prediction from the gynecologist that I would have six months to live. He was appalled.

"You did great. You are a powerful woman," he replied. I tell my students to be careful about giving any early diagnosis when something is not proven. I have heard of people committing suicide, getting a divorce, or getting themselves in massive debt when they hear that they only have a certain amount of time to live. I am glad that you didn't do anything like that."

I got upset and angry.

"Let me help you and your students understand what a real story is when someone is given an unproven cancer or brain tumor diagnosis: I have taken stock of everything and everyone in my life, and just in case I lived longer than six months, I made several decisions: I will start all over again. I will quit my job, get a divorce, and leave this city, never to be reminded again of what happened here. Aren't you happy I didn't kill myself the last two months while I was waiting for you or any of your doctors to give me feedback on those horrible diagnoses? Instead, everyone was on vacation and left me alone with a false diagnosis. You can quote me when you tell my story to your students."

I stood up from my chair and left the professor without waiting for his answer.

I called Richard the same day, telling him the good news and that I was ready to move to Munich. Within a couple of days, he had the contract prepared and sent for me to sign.

"I have good and bad news," I told my boss two weeks later.

"What's the good news?" he asked me. "Is everything all right?"

"Yes, the good news is that I am back to health and back in life," I happily answered.

His eyes lit up, full of joy and relief.

"Amazing, and congratulations. We need to celebrate that with the rest of the team. What is the bad news?"

"I'm leaving my husband and the city and want to quit my job. I am so sorry, but I will start a new life in Munich with new people. I don't want to be reminded every day of what has happened. I will start at the beginning of next year."

He looked at me in disbelief.

"You're quitting?"

"Yes, I am so sorry. I will never forget what you have done for me. I want to thank you from the bottom of my heart for everything. But it is time to move on.
I have turned the page to the next chapter in my life."

He nodded.

"I do understand. You have changed your priorities in life. Everyone who has had to go through everything you've endured in the last three months would do the same. I deeply hope you will be happy again. I am sure you will. You are strong."

Then he smiled. I began to tear up, doubting whether I had made the right decision. But there was no way back.

I left his office, closing my professional chapter with that company. The next thing on my to-do list was to call my husband in his office, five hundred miles away. I felt scared and uncomfortable because I was not good at delivering bad news.

"Hey, what's up?"

"Hey, I wanted to tell you I found a new job. I am going to move to Munich."

"What? Why didn't you tell me before? I am sure there was a longer process of interviewing you till they finally offered you the job. You and I should discuss such a big decision first. Why didn't you ask me what to do? I am your husband. We need to make the decisions together." He was upset.

"Well, not anymore, Jim," I replied.

My heart was pounding. I didn't want to hurt him; he wouldn't understand why I decided to leave him.

"I will file for divorce."

Silence.

"Hello, are you still there?"

He hung up.

He refused to talk to me for several months. I organized my relocation to Munich and tagged his belongings for a separate truck destined for the city where he lived then. Both trucks arrived on the same day.

Six months later, Jim called, asking me to come back. I said no. He did not understand why I had left, blamed me, and accused me of destroying the marriage. He couldn't understand what I had to go through. We got legally divorced three years after our wedding, precisely on the same day and at the same hour, 11:00 a.m.

He didn't show up. I wouldn't meet him again until fifteen years after I left him.

The doctors never could figure out why my hormones got out of balance to such a degree. I decided to rely on a natural healing process for my body and stopped taking my doctor's medications at my own risk. He wanted to get me tested monthly, quarterly, and yearly to ensure I was okay and on the right track. I was anxious, but I wanted to try it. I hated it to be dependent on pills for the rest of my life. Two years later, my body was in balance again.

I had a whole new life. I felt like celebrating my birthday again. Everything had changed since I got that call from my gynecologist six months earlier. My view of the world changed. My perception of myself changed. It didn't matter to me if I was married, whether I was considered a career woman, or whether I fit any of the labels society puts on single women. I wanted to do the work I loved. I wanted to be with people who appreciated and respected me and were my people.

My health was the only thing that mattered. Nothing else was important anymore. I left my past behind and started all over again.

Story 3: My Mother. Why I left her.

1 9 9 1

Thirteen years after returning from Iran, my plans to build a family while having a management career in the corporate world hadn't worked out. I was divorced and childless, but at least I had a successful career at a well-known US corporation. I loved working at this company and was appreciated by many. I was respected as a professional manager and happy in a new relationship. My male colleagues respected me, and we liked working and being together. I didn't miss anything at all. I did my job and performed very well. My mentors supported and advised me, and I got promoted to the next career level.

On Thursday, a beautiful sunny morning with a dark blue sky at Lake Starnberg near Munich, I had no idea my perception of my life was about to change. I got up, opened my hotel room window, and breathed fresh, clean air. Amazing. *It's another gorgeous day in paradise*, I thought. The sun had just risen on the other side of the lake, greeting me and the landscape in beautiful sunlight.

A few days before, my marketing colleagues and I had checked in to a management workshop at the La Villa, a gorgeous boutique hotel on the lake. The architecture reminded me of an old Tuscan villa, styled with terracotta stones and a lavish garden with pine trees spreading downhill right to the shore of the lake. The interior design was quite contemporary, with lots of modern art on the wall.

I put on my bathing suit, walked downstairs, and jumped into the lake, enjoying the crisp air and cold water to clear my head from the previous dinner party, where I'd had too much wine. As a group of managers, we enjoyed working together and having a lot of fun at the same time. It was amazing. Later in my career, I never again experienced the same joy of spending time with my colleagues 24/7 as I did in this group. We were successful partners in crime with an extraordinary team spirit.

I was grateful to have such amazing colleagues.

After a quick swim, I got out, covered myself in a big, white, fluffy towel, and looked over the lake while standing barefoot on the lawn. There is nothing better than that on an early summer morning. I returned to my room, showered, dressed, and walked to the seminar room to grab a coffee.

The workshop was led by a famous management trainer, Jack, who held a mirror to your face and encouraged you to look deeper into your heart, soul, and mind. Dealing with our demons, blocked mindsets, prejudices, long-buried desires, and unconscious habits was challenging and demanding. But it was worth it for those who dared to open their eyes and hearts. I realized the masks everyone wore and the roles they played, including my own.

That morning, Jack was already in the room, preparing some flipcharts. He was an early bird, too. He ran every morning, and I swam. I enjoyed having a quick chat with him, more informally and a little flirty, before my colleagues arrived.

I like tall, slenderly built athletic men who are intelligent, easy to talk to, witty, handsome, and know how to dress well. The combination of these traits has always hooked me.

The topic of the previous two seminar days had been to self-reflect on who we were and who we had become as human beings and in our careers. That day, Jack called our final exercise "deal with your unfinished business."

None of us had heard the term before. "Unfinished business" was defined as any hurtful or traumatic experience, usually with someone who meant or meant a lot to us. Such experiences create painful thoughts and nagging emotions. Jack explained that they remain stuck in our bodies, hearts, and minds until those hidden thoughts and feelings have been put on the table, discussed, expressed, and forgiven. "The price is high if you don't work through these," he said. We would block ourselves from a life of free spirits—physically and emotionally. Unconsciously, we would be shackled to the past when we wanted to move on.

That afternoon, our task was to identify one major topic as an "unfinished business," write it down, think about what we could do, and present it to the group the next day. The goal was to become free from those grudges, anger, regrets, and other nasty emotions from our pasts. We had only a quick dinner break that evening, then were commanded to spend the evening alone, without any distractions like wine or chats with our colleagues. The task was to think about a significant issue with someone from the past that we had never talked about or resolved with that person. After the dinner, everyone disappeared into their rooms.

I went outside. It was a warm summer evening with a nice breeze from the lake. I found a bench under a tree overlooking the lake. I sat down, took a deep breath, and opened my journal. It felt scary to see so many white pages staring at me. What should I write down? I had no idea. Various fights with my sister or my ex-husband came to my mind. Still, none seemed worth labeling "unfinished business." I watched what was happening on the lake. Some birds were fighting with each other, some ducks were looking for a place to stay overnight, and several boats sailed by. It was mellow and peaceful. I wanted to join them for a sunset sailing ride rather than sit here and think about my unfinished business.

But the universe had it all planned, obviously and as always. Out of nowhere, I suddenly heard my mother's voice. For many reasons, I hadn't seen or spoken to her for twenty years. If anything important in my life could have been described as "unfinished business," it would have been my relationship with her. I refused to see or speak to her because I felt deeply hurt by her behavior and the words she said to me when I was a child and teenager. I had been heartbroken and angry all these years. I felt an intense rage every time I thought about her. I hadn't been able to forgive her for twenty years. Often, I woke up at night angry and upset because I had dreamt about her.

My mind wandered back to when I was a teenager living with my mom and sister after my parents divorced. Memories started resurfacing. I felt like I was sitting in a movie theatre, watching a film about me, looking back on my childhood and teenage years.

*   *   *

My mom was seventeen when she gave birth to me and nineteen when my sister was born. She was tall, five feet eight inches, with brown hair, green eyes, and a feminine, curvy body. Her role model and favorite actress was Sophia Loren from Italy. She copied her by acting like Loren's characters from the sixties and seventies movies, with her charming attitude, body language, and style.

Nonetheless, I hated everything about her because she wore many masks. Her voice, body, how she walked and talked, dressed, and drama-queen attitude were roles she played to grab attention from everyone around her, attracting men nearby with her flirtatious behavior. It was obvious that men were attracted to her, too. Back then, it seemed she was the fairy-tale woman who drew men like moths to the flame. I didn't understand why, but people told me she appeared charismatic and charming.

Only my sister and I knew that she was the devil in disguise. When she was still married to my dad, we lived in a big bungalow-style house with a ten thousand-square-foot garden full of trees. After the divorce, she showed her real character: a grimace full of anger, hate, jealousy, egoism, and pride. She was lazy, didn't want to work, and didn't care about my sister and me. She treated us as adults and made us take responsibility for our lives, even as twelve-respectively fourteen-year-olds. She didn't make us breakfast in the morning and instead gave us money to buy a roll at the bakery. She didn't care.

When I would return from school, I had to cook lunch for my sister, herself, and me, clean the house day in and day out, and do everything to manage daily life for the three of us. My sister got away with not doing most of the work by a trick: she cared for our mom whenever she felt tired, sick, or alone. My sister showed empathy and comforted her. She was smart. I couldn't pretend to care for her because I was the housekeeper. I thought this should be enough, but it wasn't appreciated.

During her pretended sick days, mom stayed in bed all day, asking my sister to bring her something to drink, eat, get medications from the pharmacist, or entertain her by talking without stopping. Our life was all about her.

She also didn't give us money to buy clothes or books for school. She blamed Dad for not paying her enough for us. We had to earn money by working somewhere in the afternoon or during summer breaks or holidays in spring. I worked many jobs in the afternoon after school, such as babysitting, working at an assembly line for perfumes, and working as a shop assistant in a fashion boutique and a chocolate store. I remember one job I did with my sister where we worked for a carton manufacturer, folding paper cartons. Our fingers and hands bled in the evening from the papercuts we got all day.

After the divorce, my mom had a full-time job and received monthly child support from my father for my sister and me. But my mom used all the money to continue her affluent lifestyle with men, travel to casinos, and stay in luxury hotels on weekends. She lived beyond her financial limits.

*　　*　　*

My dad worked in foreign countries all his life. On average, I saw him only once a year while my parents were married. After they got divorced, he married another woman four weeks later. Her name was Anna. She moved into our spacious former childhood home with her sister and niece. My sister, mom, and I moved into a two-bedroom apartment nearby and had to give away our beloved German Shepherd, Polly. After the divorce, my dad didn't contact us again, and my mom did not allow us to contact him. She was my parental guardian, and I was supposed to follow her rules until I turned twenty-one.

Nevertheless, I loved my dad, although I rarely saw him at home while they were married. He was about six feet tall, had dark, short hair, and a beard around his chin like Lenin, the former Russian dictator. He worked as an engineer who built manufacturing plants in foreign countries. He came home only once a year, sometimes even less. Whenever he was home, he brought gifts for my sister and me from the countries he had worked. He purchased jewelry made of silver and gems, brought carpets from Persia, suede coats and boots from Turkey, silk fabrics and shawls from India and China, and even an original silver-coated samovar from Russia. Occasionally, he sent a recorded tape with messages to ensure we were fulfilling our duties, i.e., helping our mom, studying, and getting good grades from school. I adored him from far away. I put him on a pedestal. He was the only one who saw and appreciated me, cared, and listened. He pushed me in school and encouraged my efforts. It was essential for him that my sister and I would get a good education, go to university, and get a degree. High-level education was crucial for living a decent, wealthy, and value-oriented life in the mid-twentieth century. He had finished three different engineering studies with a master's degree: construction, measuring and control technology, and chemistry. He was one of the top five engineers in the world, and he was booked for special engineering projects worldwide.

He swore he'd turn me into a smart girl, hardworking and intelligent enough to attend college and get an academic degree. Doing so would make a difference and allow me to be independent of anyone.

"Whatever you study and learn, no one will ever take away. You will always get back on your feet and can start again when you are in trouble. You will be independent of any man's money because you will have your own funds."

In repeating these words, he left marks on my heart, life, and professional path. Learning became a never-ending project, no matter which career level I achieved. I loved making my dad proud. His parenting was very strict. He instilled in my sister and me the core values of good manners, mindset, and being respectful with polite behavior toward others. We could not get away with anything, like lying, not asking for approval before going somewhere, or overstepping somebody else's boundaries. He never beat me but always encouraged me to do the right thing. He translated his experiences while working abroad into valuable advice that helped me survive in dangerous situations. I wouldn't say I liked it at the time because his teaching approach felt like a drill in a military camp.

I was anxious about making mistakes or not being good enough. But I also wanted to live freely, be a free spirit, and do what I wanted. Later, I realized that his strict upbringing and insistence on values, manners, and habits would provide a solid base and structure to carry me through good and bad times.

*   *   *

1 9 7 1

I had to do it alone.

I was sitting on my bed reading my favorite book in our tiny two-bedroom apartment, which I shared with my sister and mom. I was a sixteen-year-old girl who desperately wanted to leave this place called home. For me, it was hell, and I missed my dad.

"Gabby, where are you? Lazy girl, I need you in the kitchen. Come here, immediately!" my mom commanded. For most of my childhood, I remember, she yelled at me, beating me with everything she had in her hands and for seemingly no reason, just for the mere existence of being my dad's favorite daughter. She was jealous. Back then, I didn't understand why. She needed to control me, my mental energy, curiosity, willpower, and intelligence, because that's what drove her crazy. Daily, we fought because I wanted something different from what she wanted me to do or be.

My dad loved my leadership energy and often told me I was smart and his beloved renegade. On the back of a photo of myself as a four-year-old, he wrote *our staff sergeant* and added a smile. I had been running around all day, discovering my environment, and had fallen into a water supply well and had to be rescued. I was balancing on top of tall brick walls and fell off, hitting the back of my head twice. I was carelessly playful, full of energy, curious about everything, and adventurous. My mom couldn't handle me.

After my parents divorced, my mom's aggression and violence toward me worsened. I was the one who painfully reminded her that he had left her. One day, she told me, "You are why my life has become miserable. If I hadn't gotten pregnant with you, I wouldn't have married your dad. And now, I am divorced and have no money, which is a shame. It's all your fault. I would have been much better off and happier today if I had aborted you or if I had raised the placenta instead of you. I will send you to a foster home for children who misbehave."

I was shocked and started crying. I didn't want to go into a foster home. I had heard about places where children were tortured and sometimes beaten to death.

When she realized that I was scared of her threat, she sadistically pushed my button even more often. She had no emotional control over her violent temper nor love for her two daughters. For sure, I was not loved or welcomed at all. Often, she admitted that she was suffering from intense mood swings, from heavy depression to sky-high joy, within a couple of minutes. Little did I know back then that she was a narcissist and would have been diagnosed with bipolar disorder today.

I felt like I was the representation of Cinderella in the real world. I was in prison that I could not escape from. I was still too young to become independent and live my own life. I was desperate because there were so many years to go until I would turn twenty-one and finally be legally perceived as an adult and allowed to check out from home. I endured endless days, weeks, and years that did not seem to move forward, like sitting somewhere on a hot summer night without any breeze.

Can't she leave me alone, at least for an hour, without asking for anything?
I thought, sitting on the bed, reading my favorite Mark Twain book, *The*

Adventures of Tom Sawyer. I daydreamed that I could be Huckleberry Finn and live a free, adventurous life in nature without any obligations.

My mom opened the door to my room and looked upset.

"What are you doing here, you lazy girl? Again, you are reading. Come into the kitchen, prepare dinner," she demanded harshly.

I looked up from my book straight into her eyes.

"Yes, I am coming," I replied quietly with my poker face. I never wanted my mom to see me vulnerable again. This kept me safe from her violent attacks.

Before I followed her to the kitchen, I wanted to ask her about the missing money I had saved from my jobs and hard work at the assembly line for three weeks during my school break. Maybe she knew where I put it or had found it.

"Do you know where my money disappeared to? I remember putting it in my nightstand drawer, but it's not there anymore. I looked in the closet but couldn't find it there either. Do you know where I could have put it?"

I opened the drawer.

"Look, Mom. I put it right here." I was concerned and confused.

Silence.

"Have a look in the drawer. See, it's gone. I saved all the money I worked for during the last six months. It was quite a lot of money."

I paused and looked at her, repeating what I was saying.

"I put it right here, but there is no money anymore. See, it is empty. I don't understand. I have searched everywhere. I might have put it in the closet, but it isn't there either."

I was almost crying. It was so hard, working right after school, keeping up with the household chores, studying for school exams, and many other things I had to take care of.

"Maybe I lost it on my way to school, or my sister took it?"

I was thinking aloud, somehow perplexed. My mom stood tall at the door and didn't want to come to my nightstand or investigate the drawer. Instead, she glanced at me with a frozen, stone-like facial expression.

"It's about time you pay your share of the food and rent here in my household, young lady. I am not willing to pay you anymore. You are old enough to make your own money. It's best if you leave school and look for a job."

It was like someone had pulled the rug right under my feet. What? I could not believe what she was saying. I was holding my breath.

"Come into the kitchen and help me—right now!"

"Did YOU take my money out of the drawer? You stole it!"
I yelled at her for the first time in my life.

My face turned red, and I could hardly breathe. I was devastated. She had taken my hard-earned money without telling or even asking me. It was my money. How dare she? I felt nothing but anger, rage, and mistreatment. It never occurred to me that my mother would steal my money out of my drawer. I had trusted her fully. She abused my trust and honesty and couldn't care less. She killed the rest of my love for her.

"When did YOU do that?"

My voice was choked, and my heart pounded. Anger was creeping up from my heart into my throat. She must have taken the entire amount while I was sleeping because she usually left the apartment earlier than I did. Or did she take it out while I was working? Maybe. I had no clue. I felt queasy.

She had stolen my money. My mother was a thief, betraying her daughter. She could have asked me for a share of my money. Maybe it was a power game for her. I didn't understand what was going on.

For years, she had received significant monthly payments from Dad for me and my sister. She had already received half of the value of the big house in cash from him. Together with the salary from her full-time job, how could she not cover our expenses?

How could this happen? She hadn't paid for clothes or books for me in a while—only stuff for my younger sister and, indeed, for herself. She didn't even need to pay for food for me because my boyfriend's mother had invited me for lunch and dinner—every day for five years, even on Saturdays and Sundays. I appreciated being welcomed by them because I felt cared for, loved, and protected. I am forever grateful to this woman for watching over me and feeling valued by her without any judgment. She knew our mom worked full-time and didn't come home most evenings. My mother didn't even care, nor did she thank her for being so kind to me. She didn't attempt to give anything back in return, not even flowers—no sign of appreciation or respect. I felt ashamed having such an unpolite and ungrateful mom with no decent upbringing.

What did she do with all the money? Why did she need so much on a daily base?

I saved as much as possible while working in the afternoon. I didn't want to burden my mother, but obviously, it wasn't enough. She spent more money than came in.

Years later, I remembered that she would travel to different hotels in Germany for years. It dawned on me why she needed so much money. My mother was a gambler. She was addicted to the world of casinos and spending time with her different boyfriends in luxurious hotels. Every Friday, she left the apartment to drive with her latest lover to a casino, where they played at the roulette table and stayed overnight at a nice hotel. My sister and I had to accompany them, spending the weekend in the hotel room. Most of the time, she must have lost money. For more than ten years, gambling in casinos was one of her favorite hobbies, along with horseback riding. That's why she needed more money than she got from my dad during their marriage and what she earned in her job after their divorce. Still, she kept gambling during the weekends.

The day I realized she had stolen my money, I discovered she had bought a new dress. Now, I knew who paid for it. I felt deceived. I was shaking emotionally and physically. I was overwhelmed by a mixture of anger, betrayal, disappointment, sadness, and even grief.

I lost my trust in her completely. I felt abandoned and alone. I could barely sleep that night. I fell asleep, woke up from horrifying dreams, and fell again. I was exhausted emotionally. Two days later, I ran away from home and stayed with a friend at their house. It was the first time I had run away, and it wouldn't be the last time.

On Sunday, my mother returned from her trip and was searching for me. Finally, she found me at my friend's house. She took me home, blamed me for escaping, and beat me up. She hit me in the face, left and right. I tried to cover my head with my arms and hands, but she was stronger. It hurt terribly, but fortunately, my feelings became numb quickly because she had beaten me so many times for years before. I had gotten used to it. She threatened again to send her to a foster home for difficult children far, far away. I was scared.

I sighed. My boyfriend and his mom took better care of me than my mom. After a while of being threatened but not brought to a foster home for children, it dawned on me why she would not throw me out of my house. If she did, my father would stop paying her the monthly alimony for me.

Well, I couldn't sit by any longer. I wanted control of my life. It was as if I lived in another world. Whatever I said or did was wrong. I had too many bruises on my body from being beaten using the umbrella, the riding crop, or whatever she could get in her hands—even an electric iron one day. These were the stories of my violent and abusive mother throughout my childhood and teenage years.

One day, my sister saved my life when she got between me and her, who, in her rage, had picked up a heavy floor vase to smash on my head. My sister was screaming, and I pushed her aside till she let go of me. My mother was hazardous to the world, especially to me. Anything was better than living in this hell, my so-called home. The marks on my body healed over the months. Still, the scars on my heart from her emotional abuse took decades to forgive, but they are never forgotten.

I longed for a mother who cared for and protected me—a heartfelt wish never fulfilled. No matter what I tried, legally, I was too young to start my life as an adult. And now, since my mother stole my savings out of my drawer, I didn't even have enough money to leave secretly in the middle of the night. In the '70s, women had to ask their husbands to open a bank account, or, in my case, I would have had to get permission from my mother (which she would never do) or my father. Living alone in an apartment was not appropriate for a "good and well-behaved woman," and certainly not for a teenage girl. My reputation as a decent lady would be destroyed.

I had no choice but to stay with her. Having been raised in the mid-twentieth century, my mom wanted a traditional, conservative life for my sister and me, meaning marrying a wealthy man and having children. She taught us everything to become pretty wives and properly manage a household, including cooking on a sophisticated level of French cuisine.

She also taught us how to look for and select a wealthy husband. I didn't like it because I didn't like manipulating people, nor did my sister. I was looking for true love and care, not to be a gold-digger.

My beloved sister and I did the opposite of what she tried to teach us. Instead, we both became successful women in our careers. My sister never married.

As a teenager, my mom allowed me to spend time with boys and girls my age from our Lutheran church. She even let me go on vacation with the church group I was a member of. The pastor chaperoned the road trip to the Atlantic coast in France. Mom thought that I would be safe in God's hands and wouldn't get pregnant with the pastor on my side. Except, I fell in love for the first time. Matthew was eighteen, with dark hair, a slender body, a gorgeous face, and the coolest guy in our little town.

When he broke up with me several months later, I was deeply heartbroken. I couldn't stop crying; my body shook, and I banged my head against the wall so as not to feel the pain in my heart but in my head. For the first time, my mom seemed to care about my feelings and what I was going through. She didn't hug me but tried to talk me out of my pain.

"This young man won't be your last boyfriend in your life. Forget him. He is not the love of your life, just the first one you fell for. Other mothers also have great sons. Time will heal everything. Just forget him. He is not worth your tears."

"How dare you? I love him!" I sobbed.

When she realized those words would not change my grief, she changed the strategy to get me out of my heartache. "I have an idea. I will tell you how you will get your boyfriend back."

Suddenly, a little beam of hope touched my heart. Within seconds, I felt excited and much better.

"You will have a party here in our house. You will invite all your friends, including him," she said.
"Okay, and then? How am I supposed to get him back?"

"I will tell you shortly before the party starts. It is important that you feel confident and happy from the inside out. Thus, we will dress you up. You need to wear the most beautiful and fancy dress that evening. You should feel proud of yourself."

"Oh wow... that sounds amazing." I was in awe and got excited. I became curious about her secretive attitude and what she wanted to teach me.

"Invite all your friends to our house. The more, the better. Four weeks before, we will send out written invitations with the date, time, and RSVP so we will know how many will attend and can do the planning."

A week before, she bought me a fabulous dress. I loved it. It was the latest fashion and the fanciest dress I ever wore. It was a '70s-style jumpsuit without sleeves and with extra wide legs at the bottom—all made of white crochet. On the day of the party, she showed me how to put makeup on. I felt exceptional, and for sure, I looked very different than in my normal appearance. Then, she told me exactly what I had to say and how I had to behave during the party, especially concerning Matthew.

"I want you to be self-confident. Matthew should realize that you don't care about him anymore and are not suffering because he dumped you. Understood?"

"Yes…" I had no idea what to do or how to behave like that.

"When he arrives, you greet him as you greet all others—no special affection or treatment for him. Treat him like everybody else, or even better, a little less kind. You simply give him a cold glance. You can be a little arrogant toward him, too. Don't show any appreciation for the fact that he finally showed up. It would help if you kept your distance. He is not allowed to touch you or kiss you. When he comes to talk to you, leave him and walk to another friend. Don't get into a conversation or discussion with him. Be proud! Show him that you know you are an extraordinary lady. That will make him regret his decision to dump you. You will see it won't take long before he approaches you to get you guys back together. Depending on how you feel, you go from there."

I was stunned. I expected her to recommend I behave differently. I remember it all as if it happened yesterday.

My ex-boyfriend and several other people arrived at our house right on time. Nobody arrived late. They were very curious about how I lived. Compared to their homes, we were considered affluent since we lived in a large house with a garden and a big dog who guarded us. I was excited, nervous, and happy at the same time to be able to host my friends.

When I opened the door, I did not expect to see all my friends arriving simultaneously and Matthew standing right in front of it.

"Hey, everyone, you finally made it. Welcome!" I smiled. "Come on in. The party will take place in the basement. Just follow me!"

Matthew tried to kiss me on my cheeks as a hello, but I turned my head away and moved aside.

"Come on in, everyone," I called while waving my arm to usher them in.

We lived in an L-shaped bungalow, around twenty-five hundred square feet, with four bedrooms on the first floor, an entirely constructed and furnished basement with four more rooms to use, a big party room, a fully equipped wet bar, and a ten thousand-square-foot garden.

With lots of "wows," they followed me through the lobby, glimpsing into the other rooms and the basement. They looked around with big eyes, wondering about the space we lived in. I led them down the stairs into the basement and our party room. My mother had already prepared a buffet of snacks and sandwiches and had stored some soft drinks, beers, and several bottles of wine in the wet bar. She had brought down her tape recorder with pop music to play. She quickly appeared on the scene to welcome my friends, quietly reminded me of the time the party should end, and then left.

It was hard for me to be unfriendly and inconsiderate to my ex-boyfriend. As advised, I chatted and laughed with everyone else except him. Now and then, I secretly looked over at him to see what he was doing. He was talking with some other boys, holding a beer bottle. Often, I felt his eyes on me, watching me while I was busy serving my guests. I stayed strong. I didn't respond at all but showed him my cold shoulder. I stuck to Mom's strategy. In doing so, I realized that I had my emotions and hurt feelings under control. I didn't feel weak or inadequate any longer.

A couple of hours later, I had to go into our kitchen on the first floor to pick up some more beers. When I walked back, opening the door to the basement, I saw Matthew sitting in the dark, blocking the stairs with his legs.

"Would you mind letting me pass? I need to take the beers to my guests," I said to him, as cold as possible.

"No. I want you to sit next to me. We need to talk."

"What do you want to talk about?"

I kept standing with the beers in my hands, my heart pounding against my chest. I feared Matthew would become angry because I had acted impolitely toward him.

"I want us to be together again. I miss you, your laughter, you being you. I miss our walks and spending time together as a couple. I apologize for what I said and did, for questioning you and us, and for dumping you. I am sorry."

"Well, that surprises me. I don't know what to say. Let me think about it. I will take the beers to my guests and then come back. We can talk then."

I replied using the best poker face and voice I was able to. Internally,

I was leaping for joy. I walked down the remaining stairs with the beers, hands shaking.

Don't stumble or make embarrassing moves while grinning from ear to ear.

Ten minutes later, I went back to the stairs. Matthew was still sitting there, patiently waiting for me. I didn't say anything but kissed him on the cheek.

"What does this mean? Is this a farewell or welcome kiss?" he looked at me anxiously.

I laughed, grabbed his hands, pulled him up, and squeezed him. I was on cloud nine.

My mom's advice had paid off. She knew how to deal with men, even with an eighteen-year-old young guy. I got Matthew back.

Although I was happy to be back with Matthew, the experience changed my view of men. I wasn't sure what exactly had changed, but I was confused. I had manipulated him, and it had been too easy. I wondered whether he would have the same intention to get back with me the following days after everything was normal again when he wouldn't be under this "spell" my mother had helped me cast.

Another lesson I learned was how to gain control over people. It scared me—I didn't like being able to do that. I didn't want to control other people, but I learned some rules about power games.

I felt it was wrong. I wanted someone to love me for who I was, not how I behaved or dressed. Had he returned because he truly loved me or because I ruffled his ego while mostly ignoring him? I was not sure anymore. I decided that if I could manipulate him, any other woman could do that, too. One day, he would cheat on me because another beautiful girl would try to seduce him. I didn't want to become a jealous control freak like my mother. My feelings for him faded away. I slowly withdrew and left Matthew three months later. We never really talked about breaking up. We just stopped talking to each other and finally didn't date anymore. He seemed okay with it, making it easier for us both. No discussions, no fights.

Later that year, we met several times at friends' parties. It was okay. We each had new lovers. He had found a new girlfriend, and I had discovered a new boyfriend. Benjamin was twenty years old and a political economics and sociology student. Six feet tall, he was a very intelligent, widely read hippie of the early '70s, bearded type with long brown hair. I liked him. So did my mom. She wanted to meet and talk to him about the seriousness of having a relationship with me. My mom invited him to our apartment one day but asked me not to participate in the conversation.

"I want to check him out, what he is up to, and whether he is serious about you. I don't want you to experience the same disaster as with Matthew."

"Okay. No problem." I was okay with that.

Benjamin told me what had happened the next day when he met my mom.

"How was it? Was she friendly and interested, asking you questions?"

"She behaved quite strangely."

"What do you mean, she behaved quite strangely? What makes you think that?" I had no clue what he was about to tell me.

"After entering your apartment, she led me to the living room and asked me to sit down. She asked whether I would care for a glass of wine or a beer.

I would have expected water or a cup of coffee. So, I asked for a beer. After serving me the beer, she played romantic Frank Sinatra music and lit several candles. Then, she sat beside me on the couch, asking questions about my studies. She didn't mention you at all, nor did she ask anything about our relationship as you have told me."

"What did she do? She wanted to seduce you?"

"Yes, I guess so. It felt like that. I felt very awkward sitting next to your mom. It was very uncomfortable. I am telling you because she came too close to me. After ten minutes, I stood up, said thank you for the beer, and left the apartment. I didn't even finish the beer. I told her that I had to go."

What had happened? I was devastated and got angry.

"Is she jealous and in competition with me? What do you think?"

Benjamin shrugged. "I don't know. If my father would do that to you, I probably would beat him up. A mother like that is disgusting."

I hated her even more, and from that second, I held her in contempt. She wanted to hurt me purposely. She knew that my boyfriend would tell me about that incident. Hearing that was terrible. It hurt. I realized that she was a careless woman with an egotistical mindset. She was addicted to not only gambling and money but also sex and attention from every man closer to her than three feet. She didn't even stop testing her attractiveness in front of her daughter's boyfriend. She had no moral constraints, values, or standards. I was overwhelmed and felt too young to deal with all of it. My body started to shake, and tears rolled down my face. I did not deserve a mom like her. I hadn't done anything wrong; I was just her first daughter. Benjamin held me in his arms to comfort me.

"Listen, your mom is an evil person. It's not your fault. A mother should never be a rival to her daughter—never even think about it, let alone test it out."

The following day, I asked her about meeting my boyfriend. "Well, he seems to be a nice guy."

"That's it? What happened? What did you talk about? About me and our future together?" I asked her, knowing what had already happened that evening.

"Nothing special. Benjamin spoke about his studies at the university."

She couldn't care less. For a minute, I wasn't sure who had lied to me: my boyfriend or her. But then I remembered when she stole my money from my nightstand. She had been a dodger and would ever be one, always. I was almost seventeen years old and decided to leave her. I had to do it alone! I had to get out of there. I had no idea how to escape that prison, but it was time to plan.

*   *   *

It seemed there was no way to meet my dad ever again. I missed him very much. After so many years, I had no idea where he was, in which country he worked, and whether he was still alive. I secretly wrote him a postcard to the address of our former house. Hopefully, he was still living there. I silently prayed that he would answer and was thrilled thinking and daydreaming about seeing him again from that day on. I hoped that he would answer my mail and, simultaneously, was anxious that my mother would find his reply letter before I would. I was sure she would have read and destroyed it without showing me.

So, I looked out of my window every morning for the postman. Whenever I saw him walking toward our house with letters in his hand, I ran to our mailbox, waiting for him to check whether I had mail. It took a while, but two months later, I got a letter from France missing the sender's address. At first, I thought it was a letter from a friend from Lyon with whom I shared notes. I grabbed the letter and walked into my bedroom.

"Who wrote you a letter?" my mother asked suspiciously and with a stern voice.

"I don't know. There is no address of a sender. It could be an advertisement or a letter from my pen-friend in Lyon. Remember?"

I knew I had to keep my secret. Otherwise, my mom would have become furious. But she seemed satisfied with my answer and walked into the living room.

I closed my bedroom door, walked to my bed, sat down, and opened the mysterious letter from France. The letter was from him, my dad. He thought and acted ahead because he anticipated my mom would destroy his letter. Thus, he had not put his name on it as the sender. I was very proud; I was sharing a secret with my dad.

To my biggest surprise and joy, he asked me to visit him and his new wife in France, where he worked. He wrote that he would be available to meet me during the weekend and that I could stay with them in the hotel where they were staying. He would book a room for me and offered several options when we could meet in August when I would have my summer break from school.

I could not believe he had responded. I was happier than I ever had been before. I had to pinch myself. After so many years, my sadness disappeared, and joy found space in my heart. I replied immediately. From my drawer in my little desk, I got some paper and an envelope and started writing him a long letter. I tried to describe what had happened those past years, having to live with my mom. I told him I desperately wanted to leave her because of her violence. I wanted to finish high school, attend college, and get a degree, but she would not allow me. Her plans for me were to leave school and find a job somewhere to earn a living. I wanted to speak with him and ask for his advice about what to do.

A week later, another letter came from France without the sender's address. Now, I knew who was writing me. My dad suggested a weekend in August to meet shortly before my seventeenth birthday. I confirmed the date immediately.

When I posted the letter into the mailbox, my visit to my dad was finally set. The next day, I told my mother. She got furious, yelling at me as she always did. I was no longer scared because I felt my dad was coming to protect and rescue me.

"How dare you do that without asking me! I knew you were doing something behind my back. You are not allowed to see your dad until you turn twenty-one! Otherwise, I will send you to the foster home."

"But I *will* meet him. You cannot and will not stop me from doing that!" I yelled back.

"Where is he now? Is he still together with his new wife? What did he write you about their life?"

"I have no idea. We will meet in France for the weekend at the end of August."

"How are you going to get there? You need money. Where are you staying? With him and his new wife?"

She shot questions at me like gun bullets. She was jealous and still heartbroken. If I had told her before and had asked for permission, she would have beaten me up and finally would have sent me to the foster home. There was no choice but to work it out without telling her details.

My heart was heavy. I felt sorry for my mom but couldn't help her anymore. I felt sick to my stomach. I almost vomited. I realized that there was no return from what I had started. I had made my decision, and I wanted to stick with it. I had to do what I had to do. No matter what she said, screaming at me or beating me up again would not stop me from traveling to France. Subconsciously, I had known it was the beginning of the end of my relationship with my mother. That's why I felt sad. I wished my life with her was different, filled with trust, comfort, and love. But it wasn't. I grabbed the bull by the horns and got started.

At the end of August, I packed a few things for my weekend trip to France. I had saved some money from various side jobs and safely hid it under my mattress so my mother would not find it again. I had learned my lesson. I had sent a short note to my dad when I was supposed to arrive in Saint-Avold, a small city in the Alsace region, close to the French border. It was a late Friday afternoon when he picked me up from the train station.

Even after four years, I immediately recognized my dad standing in the crowd of people at the train station. He hadn't changed at all. He was by himself. His second wife was waiting for us at the hotel. I was very nervous because I had no idea how he would react when he saw me. But he hugged me, then looked into my eyes, really worried.

"What has happened to you? You're so skinny. Doesn't your mother give you anything to eat?"

I didn't reply to his questions but felt greatly relieved after many years. I started crying. Now, I would be safe again.

"It's all good now. Don't worry."

He grabbed my little luggage, walked me to his car, and drove to the hotel. It was a small local hotel next to the marketplace, surrounded by several restaurants and cafés with people sitting outside. He checked me in.

"We will have dinner together in about an hour. Anna will be with us. Please be on time. We will walk to a nice restaurant. Hopefully, you will like it."

"Yes, for sure," I replied with a big smile.

I went to my room, showered, changed clothes, and an hour later, I met both in the hotel lobby. My dad introduced me to Anna; they had married right after the divorce from my mom. She greeted me friendly. She seemed to be a nice person, elegantly dressed and stylish. We walked to a small restaurant nearby and sat down to have dinner together—the restaurant was nestled in the street with ancient, low-rise buildings made of thick gray bricks. The restaurant was not fancy at all. At most, five small wooden tables with simple wooden chairs were placed on a floor made of terracotta tiles. The walls looked like they were constructed of rough concrete. Because of the ancient wood oven blasting smoke and carbon, all walls seemed dark and dirty. It didn't matter to me. To me, it was the most beautiful restaurant in the world. The owner and cook both came out of the kitchen when we arrived. They greeted my dad and gave him an affectionate greeting.

He proudly introduced me as his eldest daughter. Both men from the restaurant seemed surprised and shook my hand to welcome me. They spoke French. I understood quite a lot of what they said about my dad, who was liked and appreciated. This restaurant was their favorite place to eat, serving traditional dishes and specialties from Alsace. We sat down.

"Have you ever tried snails in garlic or frog legs in white wine?" my father asked me.

I saw the picture of a friendly little green frog in my mind whose legs were being pulled out of its body.

"No, no, and I am unsure whether I want to try that."

"You don't know until you have tried it. I will order a plate of several appetizers, and you should get a bite from each one. Then, you will know. Whatever you choose, everything is very delicious. Feel free to order whatever you want for the main dish. Just go for it."

For the first time, I ate delicious snails with garlic. I tried several other plates, and I loved them, too. My hunger crisis from the past years was over. I felt starved and couldn't stop eating.

Anna rarely said anything but watched me.

"So, tell us how you and your sister are doing. Are you okay? You can be open with everything. Anna is very much involved in the entire story of the divorce. "

"Well, I don't know where to start. Since you divorced and married again, Mom's aggression worsened, mainly against me. I haven't done anything wrong, but she's always told me I was your favorite daughter. Maybe because she hates you, she also hates me."

"Well, yes, you are my first daughter. As the oldest, your responsibility has been much bigger than your sister's. You had to take care of her, too. You needed to learn rules and how things work much faster than she needed to learn. You protected and taught her. That's why. Also, I know you are very bright and take school very seriously. You love to learn and could become one of the best in your school if you want to. How is school going now? Which classes are you attending now?"

"I am in eleventh grade and have two more years to get a degree and my university entrance diploma. I am doing okay overall, but I am best in math and arts. I love it a lot."

"What do you want to do when you have finished school? Do you want to study and become an engineer, as I am?"

"I don't know yet, to be honest. Mom has been my biggest challenge and obstacle in the last few years. She is fighting with me because she doesn't want me to go to high school, college, or university to study. She says she doesn't have the money to finance that and is forcing me to quit school right now to get a job to earn my own money. She hopes I will leave her as quickly as possible because she won't need to care for me any longer if I have a job."

"That's ridiculous. I don't know why your mom is saying that. When you and your sister were born, I bought an insurance policy for both of you to finance your college education. I have been paying a monthly fee for that insurance for the last sixteen years. The amount you are entitled to receive will cover all expenses during your time at college. Same for your sister. When both of you need that money, your mom must tell the insurance company to transfer the money to your bank account. Ask her to pay out your college insurance. You will be covered during your studies."

"Awesome. Thanks a million. I didn't know that."

I was overwhelmed. I had yet to learn about the insurance to support me and my sister in college. I was grateful to the bottom of my heart and felt relief for the second time. At least there seemed to be a light at the end of the tunnel.

"Well, I wrote you that postcard a couple of months ago because I can no longer live with my mom. She has beaten me often with her riding crop or anything she can get her hands on because she has an uncontrolled, violent temper. Every day is different. I don't know what she is up to daily, and I am scared. Sometimes, she is kind and friendly, and some days, she is furious and vengeful. I am terrified of her, anxious and exhausted. I am sure, one day, she will kill me in the heat of the moment. That's true. I am not lying or making things up."

"Yes, I know your mother. It's all good. I will protect you and your sister."

"I also wanted to write you much earlier, but she simply banned me from contacting you. She threatened to send me into a foster home for difficult children if I contacted you. She threatened to do that several times, and I didn't want to go into that place. But she has full custody, so she *can* do that, right? She can do whatever she wants to do with me. I am totally at her mercy. I don't think that a mother should treat her children like that. I think she is somehow crazy."

"So, what would you suggest? Do you have an idea?"

"I don't know, but I think it would be best if you would take full custody of me until I turn twenty-one."

"Sure, I can do that. But where do you want to live till you are twenty-one? I work worldwide—I can't take you with me. You have to go to school and should attend college in Germany."

"But I don't know where to go. I can't live with my mom any longer. I am scared to death, and I am heartbroken. I don't want to go back home on Sunday. I want to stay with you."

"Well, let me think about it. We will continue talking tomorrow."

We walked back to the hotel. I was happy and worried at the same time. I was curious to know whether I could stay with my dad. I had no idea what to do and hadn't thought through it to a preferable end. What would the future hold for me? I barely slept that night.

The following day, the three of us met for breakfast.

"How are you? Did you sleep well?" I asked my dad.

"Listen, as you have suggested, I have decided to take full custody of you under certain conditions. As I said last night, I cannot take care of you as I would like because I work in foreign countries, but I have an idea."

I was thrilled. At least my dad would take over custody, meaning Mom could no longer punish and beat me. It felt like a huge relief.

"What do you think of having your apartment?"

"Oh, okay..." I was surprised. I have never thought about that opportunity.

"But I don't have enough money to pay the rent and cover my living costs."

"I would rent an apartment for you, and you move into it. I will take care of the rent. We will buy furniture, etc., and you will start your household. In doing so, you can finish school and go to university when you have figured out what you want to do."

I was in awe. What a fantastic idea. I would be free for the first time in my life. Nobody would ever again tell me what to do or what to say, and nobody would ever beat me up again.

"Instead of paying your mother the monthly childcare payment for you, I will send you the money directly. You would only need a bank account. We can manage to arrange that, too. You could make a living. I also want you to ask your mother to pay her share to you to cover your monthly costs. It's her duty. In addition, you have the insurance I set up for you sixteen years ago. Ask her to transfer the money to your new bank account to finance your college."

I couldn't believe it. There was a plan for my future. It took a while until my dad's new ideas and suggestions settled in my mind, but I understood. After a few minutes, I started shaking my head, and tears rolled down my face. After what seemed an eternity, the vast burden that felt like a rock on my heart and shoulders slowly disappeared. I was relieved.

"It will all be good." He hugged me.

The end of the tunnel was near, with a solution I had never expected or anticipated.

"Gabby, you need to eat better. You seemed to be underweight. You are far too skinny for your height. I am concerned about you. Also, your clothes look quite shabby and worn. When was the last time your mother bought you new clothes?"

"Not in the last several years."

"Let's go shopping and find some nice dresses, so you feel better," Dad suggested.

Somebody needed to pinch me. Was it a dream, and would I wake up pretty soon?

"Wow, thank you so much. I appreciate what you are doing for me. That's very kind. Unfortunately, I cannot take new clothes home with me. My mom will be very jealous and will get mad at me again. She might throw them in the trash bin."

"Then let's buy you new clothes and leave them here. The next time we come to Germany, I will bring them and store them in our house. You will have access there at any time. That's a good idea, and you don't need to tell your mother."

"Yes..." I was gasping for air. I was profoundly grateful and silently thanked God. I was coming home. I had made the right decision to contact and visit my dad. My life had finally changed for the better. I was glad I took the initiative to escape my misery.

I left my mom a couple of months later. She didn't fight for me to stay with her. She seemed to be relieved, too, wishing me good luck. That was it.

My dad rented an apartment for me. Together, we bought new furniture, and I moved in. By that time, I was going to high school. Living alone was a real scandal because I was the first girl to attend school and still do this. It did not bother me at all. I was free for the first time and could live without fear and punishment. I committed myself to finishing school and university to start a career as an academic.

Doing so would significantly increase my chances of getting hired for exciting jobs, fulfilling my need for inspiration and intellectual challenges. I dreamt of a beautiful home with lots of space, traveling the world, and living where money would never be an issue. My academic education would give me choices and help me decide on any profession I wanted.

I asked my mother for financial support, as discussed with my dad, but she refused. She wanted me to get a job and get married as soon as possible. That was the predestined life for women in the mid-twentieth century.

"I want to study, become an academic, and start working. I won't look for a job now without a formal education. In doing so, I won't be able to earn the money I want to!"

"Find a rich man who will marry you. You don't need to study. When you finish your studies and start working, you will be in the middle or end of your twenties, too old for a man to marry you, and too old to have children. That's not your destiny and a waste of time and money, too," she spat.

"But, if you don't want to support my goals and career, I have an idea. You don't need to spend money on my education. I know there is a college fund that Dad had created when my sister and I were born. Since then, he has collected a six-figure amount each for my sister and myself to study. I want you to transfer the amount meant for me into my bank account."

"No, there is no college fund and money for you. That is a lie," she replied aggressively.

I started to sense that something strange was going on.

"Mom, why do you resist giving me the savings of the college insurance Dad has built up for sixteen years?"

"I raised you, which was very expensive. I have paid you and your sister for everything for the last sixteen years. The conversation is over."

She left the room. I held my breath and followed her.

"Did you take all the money for yourself instead of saving it for our education?"

She didn't answer, but intuitively, I knew I was right. She had dissolved the contracts and had spent the six-figure amounts meant for my sister and me solely for herself. I realized that she had used the two college funds for her private entertainment, horseback riding, and gambling trips to casinos in Germany. How could a mother do that to her kids? I always believed that a mother who loves her children would do anything to support them. Not my mom. She had done the unthinkable. She put herself first and her children last.

She was the most selfish and mean woman and mother I have ever met.

I was deeply hurt, disappointed, and furious—all at the same time.

With my dad's support, I called a lawyer and filed a lawsuit against her. I felt angry and heartbroken, but I had to do something about it. I didn't understand her horrible behavior and wanted to teach her a lesson. I wanted her to take responsibility for her children. We got into a nasty fight in front of the court.

She drew her next ace out of her sleeves when she realized she would lose the case and had to pay back all the money. She threatened to commit suicide if I forced her to pay the missing six-figure amounts.

I gave up. I didn't want to be the reason for my mother to attempt suicide. That's when I decided to shut off and leave her altogether. I cut off every connection with her and everyone around for the next twenty years.

I continued working to support myself while attending school and later university. I finished high school, studied business administration and economics at a famous university in Germany, got my master's degree, and found my first job in another city, about one hundred miles away from her. I was moving on with my life, leaving it all behind, and didn't look back, nor did I attempt to contact her again. For me, she didn't exist any longer.

I was relieved that my dad took financial care of me, at least basically. My sister also left mom two years later. She had become the target of her violent attacks after I left. Ultimately, we cut the connection for the next twenty years.

During all these years, she didn't look for us. She missed celebrating my college exams, wedding, divorce, successful management career, sharing in my fantastic travels, and meeting friends worldwide. My friends have become my second family - my family of choice.

*　　*　　*

Twenty years later, during this management seminar at beautiful Lake Starnberg, I knew the story with my mother was the "unfinished business" I had to solve. It occurred to me while sitting on the bench and watching the boats sailing into the port during sunset.

I was stressed out and tired of thinking about her, day in and day out, for the last twenty years. I wanted to understand what happened in my childhood, and I wanted to let go of these painful years. I tried to heal now and forget those memories forever.

I decided to write a short letter to my mother. The following day, everyone went back into the conference room. One after the other, we took turns in the so-called "hot seat" in front of the group, briefly explaining one personal issue, the so-called "unfinished business," and sharing with everyone what we wanted to do to solve it. When it was my turn, I walked to the front of the group with the letter in my hand. I sat down and calmly started to tell my story.

I can't remember how long it took, but it was a long time to describe the most critical parts. I wanted to justify why I left my mother and refused to see her again for two decades. The eyes of my colleagues got bigger and bigger. Some shook their heads in disbelief, and some put their hands in front of their mouths with tears in their eyes. Nobody spoke or interrupted with a question. They were in disbelief and felt my pain. My story had touched them. It was the first time in my life that I had fully opened my heart and honestly told the story of my youth as I perceived it.

"Honestly, this has been my unfinished business for the last twenty years. I have never told my story to anybody till today. It feels good to be able to share it with you openly."

"What will you do to close the story with your mother?" the management trainer asked.

"I wrote a short letter to her asking to meet and talk. I want to close that chapter in my book of life. I want to let it go and get an answer to my biggest question: Why? Why did she behave that way? Why did she do that to me?"

Everyone was nodding in total agreement, understanding, and empathy.

"But, I am still anxious. I don't dare put the letter into a mailbox. I am afraid to meet my mother. I may change my mind and won't be able to send the letter tomorrow. Thus, I would like to ask one of you to bring the letter to the post office. Then, I am sure she will receive it, and I will be forced to go through with the next step, no matter what. Whoever wants to help me with this, I deeply appreciate it."

"I'll do it."

Joe, a colleague and a dear friend, stood up, walked toward me with an open hand, grabbed the letter, and returned to his seat. It took him five seconds. I took a deep breath.

"That was fast".

I was surprised and a little in shock. The die was cast. There was no way back. It was the beginning of the end of a painful relationship with my mother. I had to grab the bull by its horns and deal with it one final time.

"I will mail it when we return from our workshop tomorrow. Two or three days later, your mom will have received the letter. In a week or two, you will know whether she will respond. I have never heard such a horrible story of a mom treating her daughter. You can let go of it, no matter how she reacts. I am sure we all wish that for you."

Everyone nodded their heads.

"Let's have a ten-minute break now. Let's open all windows to have fresh air to clean our energy." Jack asked for a short break so everyone could focus on their stories to be told.

I stood up from my hot seat. I was exhausted and sweaty from talking about the most painful years of my life. The management trainer and everyone on the team came to me, one by one, and gave me a big hug. It felt weird and awesome at the same time. I felt protected by these men. I had to go out and take several deep breaths of fresh air to collect my thoughts and focus again.

"Before we continue, I would like to thank everyone for listening to my story. I know it took a little longer, and I apologize. I am so grateful that you have my back. It's new to me not to fight alone anymore, and I am happy to have you guys in my life. Thank you so much. I appreciate it from the bottom of my heart." I bowed my head.

*　　*　　*

My mom answered my letter two weeks later. She wanted to meet me in a restaurant near where she lived. I was excited and anxious about how meeting her after twenty years would feel. I took a flight and taxi to the Italian restaurant. When I entered the place, I looked around, searching for her, but I couldn't see anyone who looked familiar. Then, I heard her voice right behind me. Without seeing her, I knew immediately who it was. No one will ever forget the tone of their mom's voice.

"Gabby, we are sitting here."

I turned around, searching the restaurant for the person with that well-known voice. A couple sat at the bar. A triple-sized version of the woman

I had in my memories sat next to a strange man, both waving at me. My mom...? Who was this person?

I could hardly recognize her. And next to her, who was that man? I must have looked shocked.

"You don't recognize me. Did I change so drastically that you cannot recognize your mom?"

Here we go again. Her accusatory voice made me feel like a teenager again. Memories of helpless hate and pain arose again. It didn't seem that twenty years had gone by.

"Well, yes. No. I don't know. It's been more than twenty years since I have seen you."

Physically, she had changed. She must have gained around sixty pounds, at least. I didn't recognize her at all, except for her voice. The voice was familiar. I walked over to them and shook their hands. She introduced the man sitting next to her as her third husband. Max was very skinny and at least twenty years older than she was. I looked at both in disbelief, but I didn't say anything. She turned her head toward Max.

"Listen, Max, Gabby and I have to talk. You stay here at the bar and order your dinner. I will have dinner with her at one of the tables. I want to speak with her alone."

She commanded him like she had commanded us when we lived together. All those horrible memories from my childhood came back. She still thought and behaved as if she were the center of the universe, the queen, and everyone had to bow to her. Even though her physical appearance had become so different, her character hadn't changed. She showed no kindness, care for him, or consideration for how he would feel getting kicked around in front of her daughter. He was a man she could push around, and he would do what she wanted him to do, like a toy. He didn't say anything but nodded his head in devotion. My mom and I took a seat at a table and ordered food. I needed a glass of wine. All my fear from the past was crawling up my throat. I was in shock. I was not prepared for this.

"So, what do you want from me?"

Her first question after not having seen me for twenty years.

"Well..."
After clearing my throat and pulling myself together, I had only one question:

"Can you tell me why you were so aggressive and violent toward me all those years? I was a child, and nothing was ever good enough for you. You constantly beat me up and threatened to send me into the foster home. You always told me I had been the reason for your miserable life, but it wasn't my fault. I was a child. I want to understand why you were so mean to me. I want an explanation. That's why I am here."

The question seemed to surprise her. She looked at me, thinking about how to answer, and after a short while, she started a story that was supposed to make me feel at ease. Hopefully, she had a rare moment of feeling responsible for what had happened.

"Didn't I tell you? You were the child I planned for? I wanted to leave my parents when I was seventeen, the same age you left me. In the fifties, the only way to do that was to become pregnant and marry a man. One day, I met your father in the company where I worked as an apprentice. He was ten years older than me, as you know. He had a great job, a good income, and a bright future ahead of him. I fell in love with him, seduced him, and got pregnant with you. We got married, and shortly after, the three of us moved to Paris, where he was working on a new project. Two years later, your sister arrived. We moved to the South of France for several years until you turned six. We wanted you to go to school in Germany."

"Okay...but why did you fight me all the time?"

"I felt alone. Your dad was traveling the world while working. He offered us a wealthy life, but I didn't know what to do with that life. So, I had all these affairs. I felt guilty, but at the same time, I was angry about your dad. He was the real cause of why I felt miserable all those years. I had to cheat on him. It was my revenge for leaving me alone at home, raising both of you. And he was cheating on me, too. He wasn't an angel as you always wanted to believe."

Again, she took no responsibility for her life but blamed others. She hadn't reflected on anything that had happened or regretted anything.

"By the way, you went to college and got your master's degree. What a waste of time. You should have gotten married and had kids. You are almost too old to have kids now. You got divorced very shortly after you were married. Why did that happen?"

"How do you know?"

"I worked for the Secret Service for the last ten years. So, I got access to your and your sister's data. I have always observed you because I wanted to know what you were doing."

"Why didn't you call us or write a letter? You are my mom. Moms do that to their children. They care for them, no matter where they are or what they do!"

She didn't reply to my question but changed the topic.

"So, how is your sister doing? I would like to see her as well."

"Can't you answer my question? I will tell my sister we have met and ask whether she wants to see you. I can't promise, but I'll put you in touch with her if she wants to."

"Okay."

"I have to go now. I will fly back to Munich very early in the morning. Somebody should call me a taxi to drive to the hotel."

"Don't you want to eat your dinner?"

"No, I don't."

I had to leave. I could hardly breathe; sitting beside her and eating anything in her presence made me feel like I needed to vomit.

She walked me to the taxi outside of the restaurant.

"Say hello to your sister. Promise?" she smiled in her well-known flirting way.

"Yes, I will speak with her. But I can't promise you anything about whether she will see you again. I know she still feels hurt for how you treated her."

"I love you."

I didn't respond, and I didn't feel anything. My mom's saying she loves me sounded so wrong and weird. It felt fake. Hearing these words came too late to do any good.

*　　*　　*

My sister wanted to see and speak with her, too. Two years later, my mother was diagnosed with cancer and died quickly. She was fifty-nine years old. My sister cared for her during her chemotherapies and other medical treatments. She repeated her role from when we were teenagers.

Today, I recognize that my mother had suffered from depression. Speaking with psychotherapists, I learned she had been a narcissist and bipolar. Her mood swings were like rollercoasters. She was a woman with a lack of empathy, compassion, guilt, and remorse who manipulated others to meet her needs. She was unaware of her behavior because she was incapable of self-reflection. She got married three times. The second marriage lasted six weeks. She seemed to have never recovered from the divorce from my dad. Shortly before she died, I was sitting next to her bed in the hospital. She told me that my dad was the love of her life and that she had always loved me.

It was all too late.

It took me another ten years of self-work, attending workshops, and training to overcome those painful memories and let them go. It definitely made me stronger.

Story 4: Lie to me

2000

I'll never forget the moment I met John. Two months before, I had decided to move from Munich to the countryside. My apartment landlord in Munich wanted me to repair several items that were already damaged when I moved in. I should have taken pictures, made notes, and sent them to her when I moved in years prior, but unfortunately, I didn't. Now, she was trying to take advantage of it and collect money from me. I was upset because I couldn't prove the damages were not my fault. I decided to talk to a lawyer, and a friend suggested that John could help me with the landlady's spurious charges.

John was a lawyer in the city with a fantastic reputation, and despite his youth, he was already accredited by the Supreme Court. I needed an expert for the conflict with my landlord, and he was the best recommendation I could get. I felt embarrassed to bother this highly qualified man with my tiny problem. But paying for the repairs would have been quite expensive. I realized he was overqualified even to look at my little story compared to the cases he had to deal with daily. Considering his hourly fee would be expensive, I wondered whether he would be the right lawyer for my case, but I wanted expert advice about my chances of winning the case. There was nothing to lose if I got an appointment and advice.

It was a lovely sunny day in the spring of 2000. I walked over the main street to his office in an alley of ancient oak trees along apartment homes and gorgeous villas near the famous English garden. It was a wealthy residential area. I remember having lived there for almost six years, driving along this oak tree–line avenue daily. I loved walking in the park, no matter which season. It was most beautiful during winter when snow covered walkways, trees, and the green lawn along the city river running through the park.

It was quite a big law office. The interior design was a mixture of old and new, combined with lots of contemporary art on the walls. When I stepped into the foyer, I was welcomed by several lawyers, busily walking around. On one of the business cards at the reception desk, I read that John ran the law office. I started to worry. I felt my case wasn't that significant to ask such high-level lawyers for advice. But I had already arrived and had made an appointment.

I learned that John owned two law offices. His assistant led me into his office and introduced us. John was in his mid-thirties, about six feet tall, skinny, and had dark hair. He wore a three-piece suit without a tie. He stood from his conference table, where he seemed to work at his laptop, walked toward me, and greeted me with a beaming smile.

"Elisabeth recommended you for my little case. She said you could advise me on how to deal with my situation," I began.

"So, where do you live?"

"I used to live right around the corner from your office, just a few blocks away. Several weeks ago, I moved to the countryside. I just realized that's the same place as your second office. It's funny that we have never met. If you want me to, I can visit your country office colleagues. I don't want to waste your precious time."

"No, no, stay. Please, take a seat and tell me what happened."

John made me feel at ease and comfortable. Maybe it was his voice, or perhaps his impressive calmness and coolness. He made me feel safe and protected in an instant. I liked him immediately. He put aside several other papers he was working on, listened to me, and looked me straight in the eyes while I was telling my story. I became nervous.

"You do nothing."
He replied when I finished talking.

"What? What do you mean? Nothing? She will take me to court. I don't want that to happen. It's not worth it, but I don't want her to get away with it. Her behavior is disgusting, unethical."

I got upset, thinking she might get away with her attempts to take advantage of me.

"Don't worry. The landlord won't. She is testing your boundaries, that's all. If you give in to it, she will get some money. If not, she wouldn't bother because she has enough money. Maybe she has nothing else to do."

"How do you know? Will your office be doing something? Writing her a letter with your letterhead? That might frighten her off."

"No, not yet. We don't do anything. We will wait for the next four to six weeks and see what will happen."

He was self-assured. I wasn't, but I had to believe him.

"Listen, you do not react to any letter or answer any call from her. I am sure she will let it go. If not, let me know, and I will write a letter. Okay?"

There was no question that he was the expert.

"So, what are you doing for work?" he changed the topic smoothly.

"I run my own marketing consultancy and training company."

"Interesting. We might need your advice."

His mobile phone rang.

"I have to take this call. It's an urgent case. I am sorry."

"That's all right. I will keep you posted regarding my case."

I stood up.

"No, no. Please stay and take your seat. It shouldn't take long."

I sat down again.

"So, what's happening? Did you find them?" He talked to someone on the other end and seemed worried but calm.

While waiting, I looked around his office. The building had been built in the beginning of the last century. The rooms had very high ceilings and beautiful stucco plastered to the top of the walls. Huge bookshelves, made of dark wood and installed from bottom to top and along the entire wall, were filled with books. The opposite plain white wall boasted a modern art piece. A grand window and a high wooden door painted in white were characteristic of a typical old but modern law office in Germany.

He hung up the phone.

"What were we talking about?" He looked at me, still worried.

"You said you might need my advice as a marketing consultant one day. That sounds exciting. I am more than happy to help you to return the favor."

"That's awesome. It would not be for this law office because we are already swamped."

"Okay. What do you need me for?"

"I have an assignment as a trustee for an investment fund. We search, select, and develop Internet start-up companies. These young men have great ideas but must learn about marketing and sales. They must figure out how to turn the ideas into promising businesses and manage a company. They must also know how to market their concepts or create brands, revenue, and profit. You could help them with that if you are interested and would like to support them."

The phone rang again.

"Excuse me." He picked up the phone.

I remained seated while I watched him talk.

"What happened?" He listened for a short while.

"Are they okay? Oh my god! Did you call the emergency and the police? Don't go away. Stay where you are until the police arrive. You have to tell them what happened. The police will question you as a suspect, so don't run away. You can leave only when they tell you to, not before. I will see you tonight. Come over to my house. We will talk then."

John hung up and took a deep breath.

"That sounded dramatic. What happened?"

"Steve, a friend of mine, is married. They have a three-year-old son. It looked like his wife and son had disappeared this morning. He knocked on every neighbor's door, but nobody had seen them. Steve saw her by chance when she tumbled out of the woods of a nearby forest. Her blouse and pants were full of blood."

"Oh my God! Was Steve's wife assaulted, or did someone try to rape her?"

"No, worse. Steve's wife killed their little son and tried to commit suicide. But it looks like she failed."

"What? What happened?"

Suddenly, I found myself in a world I had only read about in the newspaper but never experienced in person. I had seen and heard a lot in my life, including people who were brutally killed, but a mother killing her little innocent son was far beyond my imagination. How could a mother kill her child? How brutal, heartless, and cold-minded is that? I was shocked and angry at the same time.

"That's horrible. Also, for the father of the little one. She should be arrested and jailed for the rest of her life." I almost vomited listening to what he was telling me. He looked at me seriously and with a collected emotional state. "How can a mother kill a child? I mean, *her* child? Why did she do that?"

"I perceive her as being overwhelmed by raising their son. From my perspective, she is not a killer but mentally deranged, psychologically ill."

"That's not an excuse. Didn't anybody realize this? She has a mental illness. Why didn't her husband bring her to a psychiatrist? If she has a serious mental illness, she might kill somebody else. Maybe he, your friend, would be next because she probably can't handle him either? Why do you defend her? I don't get it."

"If I looked at this like you do, then yes, she should go to prison. But that would ruin her life."

"That's what she deserves! Her life is already ruined because she killed her son, an innocent child who trusted her when they walked into the forest." This discussion rattled me. I was horrified.

"Yes, but she also wanted to kill herself, which she didn't succeed in doing."

I was speechless as I listened and watched his calmness and empathy for her, maybe for him—the father. Why did he understand her mindset and behavior? If that would have happened to one of my best friends, I would have freaked out. I was already freaking out, and I didn't know anyone of them. But he kept calm and didn't seem to be concerned at all.

"Let's meet in the upcoming weeks and discuss the start-up companies I mentioned. They will need your support. My assistant will make an appointment at our countryside office, and I will show you where we are and what I am talking about."

"Okay. Thank you for your advice. I appreciate it."

I left his office, mentally scattered and confused about what I had just heard.

We had been talking for almost three hours. For days, I wondered what had happened to him, his friend, and his family. It seemed like a story from another planet, from people living in another world. That story troubled my heart.

My thoughts turned to John. How could he react that way? From my perspective, he was heartless and insensitive toward the little boy. I imagine John had to deal with these challenges and situations in his daily law practice. But in this case, it happened to his friend. He knew the mother and the little boy who was killed. He must have been shocked as well. But how could he stay calm? Maybe it was the best way to help his friend cope.

Over the following months, I visited John in his office almost weekly. He introduced me to his business partners, start-up owners, and colleagues who managed the venture capital funds. They were searching for innovative start-ups with a high potential for business success. The colleagues did the due diligence and suggested start-ups to the trust fund. Several start-ups had already received approval. My task was to develop their respective brands, define a marketing and sales strategy, and help them to execute it.

It took me quite a while to figure out what type of a man John was. Everyone adored him. He was the center of their universe. Nothing would pass without his approval or his opinion. I watched him interact with others.

He was not the typical handsome man at first sight, but he was attractive and charismatic. He was a lawyer with a brilliant mind who combined intellectual gifts with a keen intuition. His generous and bold attitude made everyone feel special and appreciated. He knew it. I asked him about it one day, and he confirmed that he was a "people catcher," and he was proud of it. John was a womanizer, too.

How did he do that? It was interesting to observe him. Although John had a life partner sitting at home waiting for him, he flirted with everyone— man or woman, young or old. It didn't make a difference. He approached people by showing affection and excitement to have met them. Everyone felt enchanted, understood, and welcomed. He would always say something kind that touched a person's heart. Usually, they were surprised, looking at him like, "How do you know?" Intuitively, he knew their emotional touch points and said precisely the right thing to make the person feel appreciated.

Why did he do that? Was he a selfless character? He seemed to want to help everyone, and he did it within a blink of an eye. John executed his charm and eloquence to an extent I had never seen before. I sensed that there was a dark side to his behavior, too. He got a lot in return. John was using his charms for lucrative business deals or sex. He wanted to be the universe's center and feel approved and accepted. He was. Always. People succumbed to his charms.

Not me. I liked him, and we had a great time working together. But that was it. In general, I keep a healthy distance from my clients.

*　*　*

I became a team member in his countryside office a few months later. I was driving back and forth between my offices. I liked being around this diverse, exciting, bright group of young people. They had a mission and were striving for ultimate success. We shared stories and discussed topics to find the best solutions. I consulted and trained those upcoming and promising start-up kids. We went for lunch and dinner together every day, including Saturday and Sunday. John always paid for every one of the members of the group. We were like family, and he was the patriarch.

It was June 2000 when John and I decided to go out for dinner without the rest of the team. He wanted to relax and be himself without the constant attention of his employees and peers. We enjoyed talking about life, goals, and future dreams during the meal.

"You told me you've had a girlfriend for over ten years and even live together. Why is it that she never shows up in the office?"

"She doesn't want to be part of it. She is fifteen years older than me and feels she doesn't fit into it."

"I am nine years older than you and twenty years older than your start-up kids. That shouldn't be a problem. They are lovely. So what is she doing all day and during weekends while you spend time with us? You don't even invite her for dinner. I am sure she would like that."

"She works as an assistant in a different law firm. I am grateful to have her. When we met, I was a student and had no money. She had a job and earned enough money to make a living for both of us. And now that I'm successful, I care for her. Shall I dump her now? That wouldn't be fair. I am paying everything back."

"That sounds impressive, but it isn't in reality. You stop her from finding and experiencing a new true love. Or does she love you so much that she endures being alone 24/7? That's called co-dependency, and it is not healthy, either. If you love her, you could pay her monthly support instead to make a decent living and give her the freedom to find the love she deserves. She deserves better than you keeping her as a friend with benefits. Don't you think?"

Honestly, I didn't know what I was talking about. Years later, I would understand what co-dependent love means and feels like and how difficult it could be to get out of it.

"Or is your ego in your way?" I continued. "That's not love. You can do whatever you want while she is waiting for you. That's very convenient for you, but she will silently die inside over time. That's not fair, and you know that."

"It's a deal for both sides. She can leave any time, but she doesn't want to."

"She can't. You provide a life that she could never afford on her own. And you don't let her go because you don't want to be alone. Isn't it? But you know what, that's not my business. I just wanted to know if she exists or doesn't exist. She feels like a ghost."

He looked at me and raised his right eyebrow. I had pushed his buttons. He took the tab as always, and we left the restaurant.

The following day, I got up and dressed. I didn't feel good, but I needed to drive to my office in Munich. I hadn't been there for several days and wondered about the mail and the journalist I shared my office with.

I thought about what I had for dinner the previous night because I felt worse while I drove toward Munich. When I entered the city's highway, my stomach cramped terribly. I had another fifteen minutes to go, and I could hardly concentrate. I got chills and started shivering. I looked to the opposite side of the highway to make a U-turn and drive back home, but the traffic was even worse over there—a traffic jam.

What should I do? I wanted to stop the car but couldn't stop on a highway. I was desperate and had no idea what to do. I called John on my mobile phone. I learned that he would always have an answer in any emergency case.

He instantly picked up the phone as if waiting for my call.

"Hey, great to hear your voice. How are you? Are you okay?"

"Hi, and no, nothing is okay. I must have eaten something wrong last night. I feel terrible, have stomach cramps, and I am shivering. I am not joking. "

"Turn around your car and return home," he replied softly. He seemed worried and happy that I called him, not somebody else.

"I had the same idea, but I can't. The traffic jam back home is even worse. I can't make it. That takes too long. I can't even drive my car any longer. Can you help me, please? Can you pick me up and take me home? Please."

"I have meetings now. Where are you?"

"I'm already in Munich and close to my office, but it will take another ten minutes to get there. I can barely focus on driving or even the traffic."

"Okay, take the next exit. Then call me and let me know where you are. I will call an emergency ambulance to pick you up. Find a place to park your car and then wait for the ambulance. Do you understand? What is your license plate number so they can find you."

An emergency? I was shocked. I didn't need the emergency ambulance. It wasn't that bad. I probably just had food poisoning.

"Well, isn't that too much? I want to return home and try to fix this food poisoning. I don't think it's that bad," I protested.

"No, no. You sound terrible. You stop as soon as possible. Call me back when you have found a parking lot."

I took the next exit, drove about a mile into the city, and stopped my car. I called John again and gave him the name of the street and the number where I parked.

"The emergency ambulance should be there in a few minutes because a hospital is nearby. Just wait and look for the ambulance. I will catch up with you later. "

I sat in my car and waited. What if they didn't find me? Had I given him the correct name of the street and the number on my license plate? I hoped so. The cramps and the shivering got worse. I started to cry. After five minutes, I saw the emergency ambulance slowly driving down the street, searching for my car and me. One first responder jumped out of the ambulance and came to my car. I opened the door. He asked me for my name and said John had called them to check on me.

"What is going on with you? Do you have pain?"

I described my symptoms to them. The other guy asked me to step into the ambulance to check my temperature.

"Okay. Your temperature is 102 degrees Fahrenheit. That's far too high.

We will take you to the hospital nearby. That's an emergency case. Please take your belongings and lock your car. You have to come with us. You are not allowed to drive your car any further."

At that exact minute, John called.

"What is going on now?"

"I don't know. The ambulance is going to take me to the hospital nearby. They told me that my temperature had already been 102 degrees Fahrenheit. I'm leaving the car and hope I won't get a parking ticket until I return in the afternoon."

"I will see what I can do. I have many meetings today, but I can send someone to get your car keys and drive your car back home. And then, we go from there."

"Awesome. Thanks a million for your support."

I was grateful that he helped me without even thinking about it. When I arrived at the emergency room, the nurse didn't ask many questions. A temperature of 102 Fahrenheit in the morning is enough information. They gave me a blue gown to wear. It was short, like a surgery gown where the back remains open. I had to turn off my cell phone, put my purse and clothes on a chair next to my new bed, and crawl into it. A simple white curtain separated the emergency beds. The nurse put me on a saline drip and asked me to wait until the medical doctor had time to speak with me.

After almost two hours of waiting, I felt a little better. I still was shivering, but the cramps had subsided. I needed to go to the bathroom, and the nurse pointed at a sliding barn door.

"It's behind that door."

I took my saline drip, tried to hold the back of my blue nightgown, and walked to the door. It was a heavy door. I could hardly open it with one hand. I opened it a little bit, and suddenly, someone fully pushed the door open. Two tall men were standing in front of me. Because I was barefoot and did not have on my high heels, I first saw two shirts at chest level. I had to look up to see who was standing before me. To my surprise, it was John and his best friend, Ed. I knew Ed from the office. A lawyer himself, he was even taller than John. Both looked at me, worried but with compassion and loving-kindness. I couldn't believe it.

"I heard that a gorgeous lady is waiting to be picked up. That's why I am here. What about you, John?"

John looked at me with deep concern. He didn't say a word.

"You guys are adorable, and I need to go to the bathroom."

They made me smile, and I already felt better.

"We will wait," Ed replied, sitting back in a chair. John didn't. He grabbed my saline drip and accompanied me to the ladies' room while I tried to keep the back of the gown together with my hands. I felt embarrassed. I didn't want them to see me half-naked from behind. John waited at the door of the ladies' room and then brought me back again.

"Your mobile phone is turned off, so I could not reach you. Thus, we drove here and waited outside the emergency area for almost an hour, hoping someone would open the door. I am glad that you did. The hospital keeps us from knowing about you. I have canceled all my meetings today and asked Ed to join me. He will drive your car back home.”

“Wow… that's amazing. You guys are brilliant.” I grinned.

I entered the emergency room and took the keys out of my purse.

“Here are my keys. Thank you so much; it's appreciated. “

“I will come back later this afternoon to check on you. Hang in there. All will be fine.” John replied, and both left.

I walked back into the emergency room, and the doctor came. After a quick chat, he decided to keep me in the hospital for a few days to investigate further what was happening. An assistant nurse asked me to sit in a wheelchair, gave me a blanket to cover me up, put my stuff on my lap, and brought me into my hospital room. The hospital was a massive old complex in a park with many green areas and benches under big chestnut trees where you could walk around. Separate buildings for each area of medical expertise were connected underground.

They brought me to the Department of Internal Medicine. I checked in and crawled again into a bed. Fortunately, I was all alone in the room, which I appreciated. I like to be by myself, especially when I am sick. The room had high ceilings and a big window opening with a view of the park. I felt weird having spent all morning waiting in a hospital bed, which disrupted my plans for the day. Meanwhile, I felt better and wanted to go home and rest there, but they declined.

“You feel better from the medication, but your condition is too dangerous. We need to know the cause of your temperature rising to 102 degrees Fahrenheit. You will meet with specialists who will examine you from head to toe all afternoon. We will know what's going on tonight. You have to stay here till then, at least."

Okay. I surrendered. An assistant nurse drove me from one medical department to the next while I was still in bed. The procedure was the same every time I visited another doctor. I had to wait, still lying in my bed. I watched very sick people come in, real emergency cases compared to mine. Nurses and doctors ran around, seemingly very busy. By late in the afternoon, I had already visited three doctors. I almost fell asleep when a nurse approached me.

"They haven't found anything to explain your high temperature this morning. You have two more visits to do today. You must be exhausted. I will bring you in, and please remain in the bed."

She walked before me to open the sliding door of the doctor's office. She turned around to grab the handles of my bed, but she couldn't. She looked confused. From behind, somebody pushed my bed forward. I turned around and looked, wondering who was moving my bed. It was John.

"Who are you? You can't do that. You can't come into the examination room," the nurse told him. She was as surprised as I was.

"I am her fiancé. I can do this." John didn't leave any doubt that he would not listen to her.

The nurse was speechless, and I was, too. I was happy, relieved, and grateful to see him. He leaned over to me: "I will never let you go, and I will never leave you alone for the rest of my life."

Maybe I already had a crush on him, but hearing him saying this sentence made all the difference. I felt overwhelmed, rescued, and fell in love with him instantly. I had come home and he had become my hero.

The doctor asked him to leave the exam room, and he did. After the medical examiniation, the nurse pushed my bed out of the room again. John was still waiting outside, right at the door.

"Where are we going next? I can do that. You tell me. I will find it," he commanded the nurse.

"No, that's not your job, but mine. You can accompany her. Just follow us." She gave him an admiring glance. As tall as he was, John looked gorgeous in his black pants and a light blue shirt with rolled-up sleeves.

He grabbed my hand and walked beside my bed until we arrived at the next department. While waiting, he sat on the edge of my bed and looked at me.

"I was serious about what I said. I have been searching for you in the hospital for at least three hours. I started at your room, but you were not there. The nurse told me where they had taken you. I walked over to the first doctor, but you had already left. I asked him where they took you after that visit, but when I got there, you were already gone. I missed you several times by only a few minutes. I couldn't believe it. It was weird. In between, I sat in the park to relax, breathe again, and think about you. I was apprehensive and concerned."

"John, you saved my life today. I am very grateful and appreciate your efforts. I am delighted that you are here now."

In the following days, John came to visit every day in the afternoon. He had canceled his afternoon meetings all week to be with me. The doctors put me on a drip feed with antibiotics in each arm for an infusion. They diagnosed an inflammation of my intestinal wall, which becomes dangerous when the wall breaks. It can kill you if not treated immediately. I became fragile in the following days. One night, I woke up because I felt queasy. When I turned the light on to drink some water, I saw that my nightgown and duvet cover had turned red. They were covered in my blood. Where was it coming from? I didn't feel any pain in my body. I was in shock. I pushed the emergency button to call the nurse. It felt like forever till she arrived.

"Oh my God, what happened?"

"I don't know. I feel terrible."

She checked my arms where the infusion needles were. One was gone. I must have taken one out of my vein while sleeping. My blood had quietly left my body through that little cavity for I don't know how long.

"This little hole is like a running water tap, except your blood is running and leaving your body. Thank God that you woke up early enough. You are lucky. Put your thumb against it so no blood can go out anymore. I will get bandages and will be right back."

She rushed out of the room and came back with lots of materials. She closed the open access to my vein and wrapped my arm with various bandages, changing my gown and bedcover. I was in shock about what had happened. It took a couple of hours before I fell asleep again.

When John visited, we were walking the endlessly long corridors and talked about everything. I sometimes lost consciousness for twenty-something seconds. When I felt weak, he caught me and held me tight until I woke up. I felt safe and protected. He saw me as the woman without the mask I showed to most people in the professional world. Once, I lost consciousness for a bit longer, he wholly carried me to my room and into my bed and called the nurse.

"Every time you lost consciousness and sank into my arms, I was scared to hell. I was frightened you would die," he confessed.

"Why are you so worried? We are in a hospital. Doctors and nurses are all around."

"It's not about that. When you called me that morning when you felt so bad, I had to call the emergency services. I was terrified that I would come too late to help you. And I am still worried about you."

"Why is that?"

"When you called, I got goosebumps, and the hair on my neck stood on end. I knew you were the one because I could rescue you. I will never forget when I was a teenage boy," he said. "I came home one afternoon and found my mom dead on the living room floor."

"Oh my God...what happened?"

"My Dad stood beside her, completely helpless, frozen like a stone, staring at her. I didn't know what had happened, but he should have called the emergency services immediately. But he didn't, and so she died. She had a heart attack. I came too late to save her life."

"I understand. If nothing else, *you* have saved *my* life and rescued *me*. That's for sure."

After a week, I was allowed to leave the hospital to go home. John was happy when picking me up. Everything changed between us that week. We had become more than friends; we had become a couple.

* * *

When I returned to work, everybody in his office and the entire building knew what had happened and how much John cared about me. His partners, colleagues, and the start-ups welcomed me back with joy. They were happy to see me again and back to health. I was lucky to be part of this caring, fantastic community of lawyers and start-ups.

The summer of 2000 was pure bliss, and everybody else in the office felt it, too, because of us. John and I were together 24/7, except when he spent the night in his partner's apartment. Weeks went by. One day, I asked him about his partner and what he had planned to do. He told me that he had already told her about us.

"She likes you. She saw you recently in a drugstore. She said that she understood, and it would be okay for her that we are together."

"What? Well, that's a surprise. I don't want to live in an open relationship or a ménage à trois. Do you?"

He didn't reply.

"You didn't tell her the whole truth, that we are together and you have feelings for me, didn't you? I understand it takes time to sort things out, but you must decide one day."

"I told her. Let me give her some time to get used to it. She and I have been together for so long. I can't dismiss or get her out of the apartment right now."

"You don't need to. Just tell her the truth. She will leave by herself and probably will move out. I would do that if I knew my partner had a new girlfriend."

Had he lied to me? Did he tell her the whole truth?

He hadn't said anything about their discussion, like what he had said and how she had reacted. I sensed that something was wrong. I didn't know what to say.

I could not imagine that he made her believe I was only an affair. Had I misunderstood what he was saying when he committed to me? The other woman was me, not her?

I left the topic alone. I was patient enough at that stage. I knew it would take time to let go of a long-term relationship; change is painful, no matter the circumstances. Humans like to stay in their comfort zones.

Every evening, we went out for dinner. Most of the time, we were accompanied by peers and business partners. John often returned to the office after dinner because he still had work to finish. His partners and colleagues usually worked and spent the evenings there until 2:00 a.m.

I didn't comment on it. This was John's transition phase, and he needed the time. It was okay for me. I trusted that it would all work out because I strongly felt we were in love, and everybody could see it when they looked at us.

*　　*　　*

My September birthday was on a Saturday that year. Instead of inviting everyone to a big birthday party, I surprised him with a short weekend trip to the South. I didn't tell him where we would go; I just asked him to pack some clothes for a weekend in the South. He was excited like a little kid and informed his best friend, Ed.

On Friday, on our way to Italy, he texted him almost every hour where we were. Everybody in the office knew I had invited him on a surprise trip. They also wanted to find out where we would go and virtually participate at every step. They were family. I told him our final destination once we drove from the airport in Naples to the port and boarded a boat to the island of Capri, built on one big rock, surrounded by the Mediterranean Sea. I had booked a famous five-star hotel on top of a cliff for the weekend.

He was stunned.

The weather was perfect—the temperature was in the eighties, a clear sky, and a cool breeze. We went to an Italian trattoria for original, handmade Italian pasta and red wine for dinner. The environment of this simple Italian terracotta-style trattoria, the loud noise of the Italian people chatting, and the scents of oleander and other flowers were incredible. I had never tasted such great pasta and local red-table wine before. I was in heaven. Later, we strolled through the village around our hotel. It was a relaxing evening that I needed after the busy and demanding weeks prior. We ordered another bottle of wine when we returned to the hotel. We sat on our private rooftop terrace overlooking the Mediterranean Sea. I was happy to be able to spend my birthday weekend with him, and I wanted to toast at midnight.

"So, who do you think you are?" he asked me quietly, breaking the silence while watching the stars in the sky.

"Who am I? What do you mean? I don't understand."

"You have everything and don't see it or even show gratitude. I think that you are quite an ungrateful person."

"I do see it. I enjoy it. I work very hard for the nice things in life and the lifestyle I like. I can afford it, which makes me proud. Why are you asking?"

"Don't you know that other people work hard as well but will never be able to afford a weekend like this?'

"Yes, maybe. But I don't believe that's my fault. Should I also suffer to show solidarity? Do you? Everybody in Germany can get a similar education and work their butt off, as I have done all my life. I deserve and have chosen my lifestyle because I have worked hard and earned every penny. I don't take anything for granted."

"You see, you are quite arrogant about your merits."

"What? Am I arrogant? Are you insane? Where is this coming from so suddenly? Why are you so aggressive?"

I couldn't believe what I had just heard. We were sitting on the rooftop of a five-star hotel, enjoying the sparkling sky and the luxurious environment, and John was bullying me.

"Do you feel bad because I have invited you instead of vice versa? It's my birthday, not yours. You don't need to be grateful, but I expect that you enjoy your time with me. Stop attacking me like this."

"Ah, you want me to be grateful for your invitation and get on my knees?"

"What? No, not at all. You are crazy."

I had to take a deep breath. Anger crawled up my throat.

The discussion went on and on. I started to defend myself, hoping John would stop fighting. But he didn't. The more I argued, the meaner he became.

"I don't understand why you are treating me like this. I hoped we would have a wonderful time here, escaping all the stress at work. You are ruining my birthday. Thank you. If you can't enjoy this divine place, you are the one who isn't grateful at all. Just leave me alone and go to hell or wherever you want. I am tired of this disgusting fight."

"No, I don't mean it like that. You are so overly sensitive. I am sorry."

Setting boundaries seemed to stop him. I was fed up. I grabbed my glass of wine, entered the bedroom, and turned on the TV. He remained outside, texting. I didn't need to ask who he was texting in the middle of the night. I knew it. It was painful to watch, too.

I was deeply disappointed about his attitude and couldn't understand what had happened. Where was the caring man I had fallen in love with several months ago? He had intentionally hurt me. Why? After a while, I turned the lights off and fell asleep. I missed my birthday at midnight and didn't hear when he went to bed.

When I got up the following day, he had already ordered breakfast and was sitting at the table outside on the terrace. The impeccable view of the blue ocean, a blue sky, and warm sunlight beaming onto the deck was the perfect start to my birthday. A massive bouquet of forty-five tall red roses stood beside my chair. John hugged and kissed me. I resisted and turned away, still disappointed about his behavior the previous night. He wished me a happy birthday, apologized for the fight he had initiated the night before, and gave me his birthday gift, a very precious watch.

I didn't believe his words anymore. He had become a stranger, and I couldn't feel the incredible energy between us any longer. I was literally on my toes, waiting for the next attack. He calmed down, made jokes, and had fun with everybody else except me.

We rented one of those Italian scooters and drove through the villages of the island. During the day, my anger grew again, and I became increasingly upset. I couldn't forgive him and rarely spoke a word. I couldn't. He had screwed up my birthday weekend. We flew back on Sunday evening. He didn't come with me into my home but returned to his current partner's apartment. I hated him even more for doing that. In my eyes, he had decided who he would be with, and I didn't comment on anything.

*   *   *

The telephone harassment began the following Monday. In the beginning, it happened just once a day. The more weeks went by, the more often the calls came in. Somebody would call but don't say a word or answer my inquiry about who was speaking.

"Hello, who is speaking?"

There was no answer, but I heard strange sounds like somebody was breathing heavily. After a while, I became afraid to pick up the phone, worried that somebody might be waiting at my door one day. I felt threatened but had no idea by whom. Whenever I got no answer after I said "hello," I hung up immediately. I realized that these anonymous calls had become part of my daily life. It wasn't only annoying but scary.

"John, I am getting anonymous calls three to six times daily. I assume that's your former girlfriend. Didn't you tell her the truth about us? What is her goal in doing that?"

"No, that isn't her. She would never do that."

"Listen, I have never received calls like this before. I am sure that's her. It's very upsetting. Please tell her to stop, because it won't change anything. One day, she might stand in front of my door, and who knows what she has in her mind to get rid of me? What if she has a mental illness like your friend's wife?"

"No, don't worry. She would never do that. That must be somebody else." He tried flirting with me to make me feel better.

"Sweety, I have a great idea. Aren't you tired of driving back and forth from home to your office in downtown Munich? Your most important client sits here, right in front of you.

"I plan to rent a much bigger office in this building here. There would be enough space for you. Why don't you bring all your office furniture here, and we can share one big room with my other law partners? It'll be a co-working space! That's the new way people will work together in the future. We will be the first to do it, and others will follow us. What do you think?"

He looked at me with a beaming smile as if he had just gotten me a big birthday gift. I couldn't resist. Hopefully, this would improve our relationship, and his ex-girlfriend would finally give up fighting for him.

"How much will that cost me?"

"The same as you pay in Munich, including Wi-Fi, etc. You would save money and time driving back and forth to your Munich office. But foremost, we would be together all day."

"Let me think about it."

*   *   *

Four weeks later, I moved into the new office space with all other start-ups, including John's team. We had a great time and invited clients and friends to an opening party. Many came. I realized for the first time that he wasn't only an intelligent lawyer for his clients but a seductive lover for many women. He must have had many affairs with women who were either his former clients or his assistants. Among them was Jessica, the wife of one of his employees in the office. Her husband's name was Peter. Jessica adored John and greeted him flirtatiously when she arrived at the party. Peter was set to come an hour later. Jessica grabbed a glass of wine, walked back to John, and whispered something in his ear. In doing that, her hands were gliding over his pants, touching his most private parts. John laughed childishly and looked at me. He saw that I saw it.

Why did he allow that? His body language spoke clearly. He liked it. They must have still been together, having an affair. Then, Jessica approached me, saying hello with a big grin.

"How are you doing in the new office community?"

I looked at her with cold eyes and raised my eyebrows.

"Jessica, how can you dare ask me? Are you even interested in my answer? You know that John and I are not only business partners but also in a relationship. I warn you, keep your hands on him. He is not your lover any longer!"

"I don't know what you mean," she replied with an innocent voice and anxious eyes.

"You know what I mean. Stop chasing my boyfriend, or you'll get in trouble. I'm warning you."

"I don't know what you mean," Jessica repeated, smiling.

"I will tell you what I mean, bitch. You might not have noticed me, but I saw you touching John's balls. That's embarrassing and disgusting, and you could have ruined his reputation in front of his clients and friends. The other guests have also seen it. Furthermore, it is disrespectful toward me. I am his girlfriend, and I won't allow you to overstep my boundaries and that of every decent woman in a serious relationship here tonight."

"No, that's not true." She tried to stay calm, but I could see she got scared.

"You are lying. I saw what I saw. I am not making things up to get in trouble with you. I am a very peaceful and tolerant woman, but you have gone too far. You better not make me angry. It would be best if you left the party. Now."

I had caught her. She started crying like a little girl because someone had taken away her favorite toy. "What? My husband will arrive in a couple of minutes. I am not going."
She sobbed.

"You better leave now. Otherwise, I will tell everyone that you are having an affair with John. Your husband won't like to hear that. You are an embarrassment to everyone here and surely to your husband."

I had spoken so loudly that the other party guests stopped talking and turned to us.

Jessica continued crying. John had watched us and came over, asking her what had happened.

"She wants me to leave the party. I don't know why," she moaned.

"I know what is going on between the two of you. And you saw that I saw you guys," I confronted him with nothing but the truth.
I looked at John. He was catching his breath.

"She has to leave the party. We are here in the office space, where I pay monthly rent. It's my space, too, and it is my right to want her to leave. Take her to the door, please."

He looked at me in surprise. Our guests stopped talking. Everyone looked at us, listening curiously to what would happen next.

John grabbed Jessica's arm and led her out to the rooftop terrace. He spoke with her, seeming to calm her down. I hated John for not having my back. Ed came over to me.

"Gabby, please calm down. I saw what you saw, too. Yes, they had an affair, but it is over now."

"Can't she control herself? Approaching him in public while I am standing next to him is humiliating. I am furious at her. What does Peter say?"

"Peter knows what she is up to. They have a so-called open marriage agreement. She can do whatever and with whom she wants to do it."

"I don't care, and I don't allow her to continue approaching my partner as long as I am his girlfriend. It is disgusting. Her husband is a wimp if he allows his wife to cheat on him." I shook my head.

I left the party earlier than I had planned. I was not in the mood to celebrate any longer. Everyone enjoyed the party that I had paid for. Could I have settled in with the wrong people - those who didn't share my values, loyalty, and integrity?

The following day, Peter came to visit me in my office.

"We need to talk," he approached me sternly. He was a little man.

"Good morning, Peter. How can I help you?"

"You cannot publicly insult my wife and ask her to leave. Why did you do that?"

"First of all, I *can* do that. I can decide who will stay at the party and who should leave because I am the main tenant of this office space. You should know the rules as a lawyer. Secondly, I had a reason to do so; every woman at the party understood. Your wife grabbed John by his balls publicly and flirted with him. I saw it. Some others saw it and were wondering. That's a no-go. I do not allow that to happen while standing next to John or in the rooms where I pay the rent for all of you."

"No, that's not true. Jessica told me already."

"And you believe her? You were not there when it happened. Listen, I am not making things up here. I have better things to do. I wanted to celebrate our opening party happily, but Jessica messed it up for everyone involved. How can you allow her to behave like that? She is narcissistic, wants the full attention of every man in the room, and is cheating on you. You better get her under control or get a divorce. You deserve a better wife than a tramp like her."

"I know that she is having affairs. It's part of our open marriage agreement. I believe you. I apologize for what happened last night, and I apologize for my wife's behavior."

"It's your life. That's up to you, but I am unwilling to accept her in our offices. Tell her she is no longer welcome."

In the upcoming weeks, I worked successfully with John's start-up companies. They had fun like a group of children playing in a kindergarten, and I was their so-called mom. I could teach them how to prevent the biggest mistakes in building a business, how important a strategy plan is, and how to differentiate brands to succeed in a crowded market.

*　*　*

At the end of October, we planned to present all start-ups at an exhibition on digitalization and e-commerce in Munich. All start-ups, including John, his team, and I, prepared the booth, many advertising materials, and events for potential customers. Everyone was thrilled.

Somebody told me my ex-husband Jim would also represent his company at the exhibition. He had become the head of sales of a very well-known brand for consumer electronic products, and this exhibition was one of the biggest in Germany. I emailed him, wondering whether he would be interested in meeting again after fifteen years. I knew he had married again and had two children. I was happy that he finally found the love of his life and started his own family. I had forgiven him and was looking forward to seeing him again. Jim was delighted to meet me, too. I didn't tell John because he had nothing to do with it. It was not his business.

We planned to meet on the second day of the exhibition in a cafeteria in the main building. Jim and I made an appointment for lunch. He had already arrived at the café and walked towards me, smiling. I looked at him and was quite surprised. I barely recognized him. He had gained quite a bit of weight and was shorter than I had remembered. He was the same height as I was while wearing high heels. His hands were small, too. Weird, I didn't remember that either.

Was this the man I had been in love with and had married? I didn't understand my decision back then. Still, I remember questioning it right in front of the minister when it was already too late.

We sat down and ordered water.

"Do you care for anything to eat?"

"No, thanks, I am not hungry. Thank you for asking," I replied.

I looked at him and could hardly hear what he was talking about. My thoughts wandered fifteen years back, and everything that had happened reappeared.

"So, how are you doing? You look great. Did you marry again?"

"No. I didn't, but I still carry your name. My email address contains your name. Already forgotten?"

What a stupid question. Somehow, rage crawled up my throat, and I became aggressive.

"Yes, I am sorry. So tell me, what and how are you doing?"

"I am running my own company as a management consultant. I advise and coach start-ups on developing and executing successful marketing and sales strategies. Meanwhile, you have become a big shot in the corporate world. Are you happy doing what you're doing?"

"Yes, it is exciting."

"So, how did you meet your wife?"

"She was the controller of the company I am working for. When we got married, she quit. Now we have two children, and I am a happy man."

He had married a controller, for sure. She would make sure to save all the money he was earning because he was very stingy with spending money.
Listening to him made me feel queasy.

"Sounds awesome. How old are your kids now?"

"The boy is six years old; the girl is three. I enjoy being a father."

"Listen, I have to go. I have a meeting in ten minutes. It was great talking with you. All my best," I said and stood up.

"But we planned to have lunch together," he replied, surprised that I was leaving after fifteen minutes. I couldn't help it.

"Yes, I know. But I have to go now. I am sorry. Goodbye."

I felt so terrible and was almost vomiting.

I left as fast as I could and rushed into the next bathroom. Thank God I didn't vomit before all these people in the cafeteria. Another woman came in.

"Are you okay?"

"Yes, I am. Thank you for asking."

I drank water from the tap and washed my mouth. I didn't expect that to happen when I made the appointment with my ex-husband. I thought I was over it because I had left him fifteen years before. I waited for about ten minutes till I had calmed down. Then, I returned to the booth with my start-up fellows and John. Nobody except John was there. Everybody else had left for lunch.

"Hey, sweety, where have you been?"

I put my purse under the reception desk of the booth and walked away again.

"Where are you going?" he asked, looking at me in awe and quite concerned.

"You are so pale. What has happened?"

"I don't feel so good. I need fresh air. I will come back in ten minutes."

I left while searching for the nearest exit and went out. I found one of the benches, sat down, and took some deep breaths of fresh air. Autumn had already begun, and the leaves of the trees around me had already turned yellow; some were even red. Then, I started to cry. I couldn't help it. It came over me from deep within. I realized that I once dreamed of being happily married and having my own family. I had finally lost my dream, which made me feel sad and devastated.

I saw John walking toward me through the exhibition exits. I didn't look at him and tried to cover up my face. He was searching for me.

"Hey, what's going on? Why are you still outside? Come back in."

He grabbed my hands that covered my face, and pulled them away. I must have looked terrible. My eyes were red, and black mascara ran down my face. He was shocked.

"What has happened? Why are you crying? An hour ago, everything was great. Who did this to you? I will kill him." He got furious.

He knew me. He knew that I was not making things up. That something terrible or sad had happened to me. He took me in his arms and tried to comfort me.

"Sweety, I told you to let me know your plans before. Who did you meet who made you cry like this?"

"I met my ex-husband for lunch." I was sobbing.

"What? Your ex-husband? Is he here? What did he say to you that made you cry like that? I will punch him in the face. Why is he here? Where is he?"

The tone of his voice scared me. He grabbed my chin, so I had to look him in the eyes. I took a deep breath to collect myself.

"He is here because this fair is also important for the company he works for. You know who it is. Please don't go over there."

"Why did you want to meet him? You have been divorced for fifteen years. Are you still in love with him?"

"I don't know. It was a mistake."

I shrugged my shoulders and looked down at my shoes. I could hardly look him in his eyes.

"I am over it. My grief is about my lost dream of being married and having my own family. It's not about him. I wouldn't think about going back to him."

"Okay, I understand." He breathed a sigh of relief.

"This will bring us even closer together. I love you, sweety."

He kept me in his arms until I calmed down. Deep into my heart, I felt the loving energy streaming to me. I was protected, loved, and seen. For the first time, I felt treated like the number one in someone's life.

"Would you please return, pick up my purse, and bring it to me? My makeup is ruined."

He laughed.

"That's right. You look terrible but vulnerable and so soft. I love that about you."

Meanwhile, Ed came out, looking for John.

"What happened to you, Gabby? Did John make you cry? Tell me. I will punch him in the face."

He looked at me, eyes wide, then at John, then back to me.

"No, no. It's all good," I assured him.

I had to smile and was grateful to have these two incredible men at my side again. I couldn't help it, I loved each one in his way.

The emotional intimacy with John had changed me to a degree I had never felt before. John behaved like my bodyguard. He was the man on my side. For the first time, I didn't have to do everything alone. It was a relief. He was right there, 24/7. I felt deeply comforted, loved, and protected.

* * *

Unfortunately, the emotional rollercoaster started again several weeks after the incident with my ex-husband. John still seemed to have many discussions with his girlfriend. He stayed at my place one night and with his supposed ex-girlfriend the next. It started to hurt that he could not make up his mind.

We discussed, fought, and reconciled, fluctuating between happiness and despair. John called me one Saturday morning a few weeks before Christmas.

"Can you stop by, please? I am in the office."

"Yes, sure. What happened?"

"I will tell you later."

I drove to our office. John was alone in the vast room with a high, curved ceiling and many desks and seating areas. He looked terrible, with dark circles around his eyes.

"When was the last time you slept?"

"I have spoken with her. It's a nightmare. She is screaming, fighting, and getting furious. I haven't slept a lot during the last week."

"So, what are you going to do about it?"

"I don't know. It's more difficult than I expected. She is blackmailing me, even threatening to commit suicide if I leave her. It's horrible."

She neither wanted to leave him nor move out of the apartment. She wanted to stay there and wait for him, assuming our relationship was a short-term affair. She had known him for over fifteen years and probably had had similar experiences with other women before he met me. Thus, she hoped he would return to her after a while. She assumed she needed only to be tolerant, sitting and waiting like a giant black spider in the middle of her web.

I loved John deeply and saw him devastated, sad, helpless. Seeing him suffering hurt me, too. I wanted to help him and be the one who made his life easier, but I couldn't.

I am not a difficult person, nor the one who pushes anyone into a relationship with me. The decision should be made voluntarily, based on love and mutual agreement. But sometimes, love is just not enough.

"Why don't you just come with me to my place? I have planned to decorate my little house for Christmas today and need some help."

"That sounds great."

This tall guy looked so fragile and needed a break. I got tears in my eyes just looking at him. He was relieved that I didn't make a scene, nor did I ask any further questions. I prepared some lunch for us, and after we ate, he helped me bring eight moving boxes from my basement into the living room. They were full of Christmas lights, wreaths, garlands, and ornaments collected over the years. I love the Christmas season. It's an extraordinary time and atmosphere, which I loved.

We placed a lot of candles all over my place, wrapped the garlands around the handles of the staircase up to the main bedroom, and decorated my antique closet, side tables, bookshelves, and dinner table. He laughed when I turned on my cute Santa Claus figure, who swung his hips while dancing to the "Jingle Bells" Christmas song.

"You are my angel. You do not know how grateful I am for asking me to help you. I am glad that I came with you. You rescued me, and my heart is yours."

*　　*　　*

He spent Christmas Eve and Christmas Day with her. For New Year's Eve, we flew to Los Angeles. We both loved being in this vibrant city and walking on the Pacific Ocean. He had booked a hotel next to the Malibu Pier. The rooms were small but gorgeous, with a balcony overlooking a full ocean view and a fireplace inside. We walked on the beach in Malibu and went shopping in Los Angeles's famous places. For New Year's Eve, we made a reservation at Geoffrey's in Malibu, an excellent restaurant on a rock over the Pacific Ocean. I was in heaven, listening to the sound of the ocean and watching the sunset while having a glass of wine and some delicious food on my plate. Could there be anything better than that?

No, not for me. Like our trip to Capri for my birthday, John couldn't appreciate the paradise we were in. After our main course, he walked out, pretending to go to the restroom. I waited five minutes, ten minutes, twenty minutes. It was almost midnight.

The waitress asked if we wanted a glass of champagne to greet the New Year. I looked at her, wondering why he hadn't returned.

"I don't know where he is. I will find him. I will be back in a minute," I told her.

I walked outside, looking around. There was no one. I went to the parking lot to see whether our car would be there. The car was still there, but he wasn't. When I returned to the restaurant, passing the bar, I saw John sitting on a bar stool with a glass of whiskey, happily chatting with the barkeeper.

"What are you doing here?"

He looked at me, slightly annoyed, already having had too many glasses of whiskey.

"What's going on with you? It's New Year's Eve, and you've had me waiting for you in the restaurant for at least thirty minutes now. Are you insane? Why didn't you come back?"

The barkeeper was surprised by what had just happened. He turned his back to give us some privacy. I was agitated to see John flirting with the barkeeper.

"Would you like something to drink?" John asked. "It's a delicious whiskey."

"No thanks. I still have my wine on the dinner table. Why did you leave me at the table, having me wait for you?"

"I just met this charismatic, handsome barkeeper. We had a great chat. Stay with us and have a glass of whiskey. The night is young. Cheers!"

"No. I want to go back to the hotel. I've had enough."

I was fed up and so sad. Two events in the year are essential to me: Christmas Eve and New Year's Eve. I always look forward to a great New Year's Eve evening, hoping for a fantastic New Year. I was crestfallen. I couldn't enjoy the evening any longer. He had crashed my little party, again, like in Capri.

When we got back to the hotel, John went to bed immediately. He didn't say anything and didn't want to celebrate New Year's Eve with me. He stated he felt terrible that his ex-girlfriend was alone in Munich. I didn't want to discuss this issue again, and I was exhausted from being with this man and his mood swings. I called room service, ordered a bottle of red wine, and made myself comfortable on the balcony. While watching and listening to the sound of the Pacific Ocean, I toasted the New Year by myself. I decided that night: for the rest of my life, I won't allow anyone to undermine my goodwill, my efforts, my happiness, or my self-esteem, ever.

*   *   *

Right after New Year's Eve, we returned to Germany. A couple of days later, I saw his car in the parking lot of our shared office space. He had packed the car with clothes, trousers, suits, and shirts on hangers. He had finally moved out and left his girlfriend. Everyone in the office was delighted to see that he had made the decision, overdue by so many weeks, even months. The ambivalent situation and emotional rollercoaster for everyone involved seemed over.

"I would like to move in with you into your home. Is that okay?"

I was surprised, and I was not happy about his request.

"It would be better if you check into a hotel before we tie the knot. That is the best thing to do. You still need time to digest your former relationship."

"No, why should we wait? I don't want to be in a hotel. I want to be together with you, 24/7."

I was ambivalent about his decision, hoping it was a final one. Although my intuition told me not to give in, I agreed. Two nights later, when we were already in bed, John got a call from his ex-girlfriend. She wanted him to come over to her instantly. He got up and left my apartment. I was upset. Three hours later, he returned, smelling of smoke from wood burning in a fireplace.

"What happened?"

"She had tried to kill herself by throwing embers from the fireplace into the trash can. I am glad that nothing bad happened. She could have suffocated. Parts of the kitchen are burned, and the walls are carbon black."

"Oh my God. Did it happen because she wasn't aware, or did she do it on purpose?"

"I guess she did it on purpose because I left her."

"That's horrible. Are you sure? Sometimes, we don't pay enough attention to our actions when we drink too much."

"That was a suicide attempt, and I am the cause. I have to rescue her. I will spend the following nights over there to calm her down."

"What? Are you insane? Don't you see that she is blackmailing you? She was smart enough to call you. She would not have called you if she had been serious about killing herself."

"You're heartless. You don't feel any compassion."

"No, I am not heartless. She did it on purpose. She is blackmailing you to make you come back to her. She knows you are the one who likes to rescue women. You can't do anything to rescue her. She is an adult woman, fifteen years older than you."

I realized he was not the man I had hoped he was. He seemed to be from another planet, and worlds separated us.

"I have an idea: you leave me and return to her. In this case, you will be a prisoner of hers for the rest of your life. Or, you face reality and take her to a shrink and into therapy. This is your life, not mine. I don't want to be involved in those terrible, manipulative, silly games. You guys are sick."

John left the following day and drove to her. He took some of his clothes and kept some in my apartment. He didn't arrive at my home the next evening or the following week. Now and then, we made dinner plans, but he showed up two hours late or not at all. Our communication was almost non-existent anymore.

I was heartbroken, felt helpless, and hated being treated like a second choice. I could hardly sleep during the night. There was no attempt or talk about whether we would still be a couple. I was alone most of the time and couldn't do anything about it again. I still hoped that he would make a decision and come back. I didn't love it, and I couldn't change it. Thus, my only option was to leave it, but that wasn't what I wanted. I deeply loved him with every cell of my body and heart. How can I try to go on without him? I couldn't.

Occasionally, he stopped by and stayed for several nights without telling me what was happening. When he spent time at my place, he often told me he had to work longer at night or go into the office early, leaving at 5:00 a.m.

I believed him, knowing the start-up gang would work till late at night. But one morning, my intuition and inner voice told me to check him out. I wanted to find him in our shared offices. I got up right after he left. I brushed my teeth, dressed, and arrived at the office at 6:00 a.m. It was still dark. Nobody was there. He wasn't there either.

I switched the lights and the coffee machine, turned on my computer, and worked on my emails. I looked up every time I heard the sound of the door. Some start-up kids came in at 7:00 a.m., and another came in at 7:30 a.m. John's assistant arrived at 8:00 a.m., looking at me in surprise. I had waited two and a half hours until John finally arrived at 8:30 a.m. He didn't even glance at my desk. He didn't see me sitting there. It never occurred to him that I would come in before him, waiting there. He walked by, carrying some shirts from the dry cleaner over his arm.

"Good morning, John. Did you sleep well the rest of the night?" I sarcastically shouted at him.

He immediately turned around, frightened, staring at me with big eyes. He didn't expect me.

"Where have you been since 5:00 a.m.?" I asked him with a friendly voice, but he could sense my anger.

"I had to go to the dry cleaner," he replied grimly.

"You are lying. The dry cleaner opens at 8:00 a.m., not before."

He turned around and walked to his desk without commenting on my sentence. He had spent the early morning with his ex-girlfriend. He made her believe they were back together again—like he made me think we were still together. I felt betrayed, and this betrayal hurt the core of my chest and heart. It felt like someone had put a knife in my heart and turned it around several times. I could hardly breathe. I didn't deserve to be treated like that.

That evening, I told him I wanted this to end and asked him to take all his belongings and leave my home the same evening. He agreed without any comment or attempt to change my mind.

The following days, I could hardly focus on my work. It had been a mistake to have shared offices. Nevertheless, we went out for dinner with the entire team almost every evening. We talked, shared stories, and laughed with the rest of the group. John ignored me most of the time, pretending I did not exist. I felt awful but didn't approach him either. My dignity didn't allow me to do that. He couldn't make the decision. Every evening after dinner, he drove back to his apartment, where his girlfriend awaited him.

I pretended to be over him and our relationship and kept calm and collected. Inside, I felt crucified and tortured, wondering what I did wrong. I didn't blame it on John anymore but on me. I had no idea why he had treated me like that. I loved him. My confidence level weakened day by day.

Obviously, his did, too. It took him two weeks to call me at home on a Saturday afternoon.

"Can we talk?"

I was relieved and anxious at the same time.

"What about? Where are you?"

"I am sitting in my car in front of your house. I have been here for an hour, hoping you would come out."

I looked out the window, and yes, his car was there.

"I didn't see you. What has happened?"

"I miss you so much."

"Do you want to come in or talk somewhere else?"

"I don't know, but I can't live without you."

He was sobbing. I was stunned yet happy that he had come to visit me. I didn't expect that to happen. I had to catch my breath. What should I do or say?

"I have missed you, too."

"Can I come in?"

I opened the door, and that was it. John's eyes were red from crying, and he looked heartbreakingly sad. He hugged me so tight that I could hardly breathe, lifted, swirled, and kissed me.

"These were the longest two weeks in my life. When we were out for dinner with our colleagues, it was so hard for me to see you but not be able to touch you. I felt terrible and anxious. Thinking that you won't love me anymore is unbearable."

I was thrilled. I had missed him, too. I was in love with him to the moon and back. We spent the entire weekend in bed. Food was not necessary. We held each other for hours; we didn't want to let go of one another. It felt like healing old wounds from all old emotional pain. We were on top of the world. Sunday evening, he called Ed and asked him to join us with his girlfriend for dinner at a Tex-Mex restaurant nearby. I was in heaven, having my favorite food, the man I loved, and his friends. It was one of the happiest weekends since we had met and been together. I didn't ask any questions.

He brought his clothes and personal belongings back into my home.

"Is that all you have? Why didn't you bring everything? I remember you had more stuff the first time you moved in. There is enough space in the closet. You must also ask the post office to forward your mail to my address."

"I will do that. Is that all you have on your mind? My clothes and my mail? It isn't on my priority list for now. You know that I have a lot on my plate. I am swamped trying to back up these start-ups' finances."

Why had he reacted so harshly? I was also swamped managing his start-ups and my regular clients. Still, the happiness of my friends and family would always be first on my priority list.

The next day, the telephone terror, which had stopped for those two weeks, started anew. John again denied that it was her. To create precedents, I put John's name on my mailbox several days later, anticipating that he had already forwarded his mail to my home address. The following night, someone destroyed my mailbox, and both our names on it were scraped off - an act of violence by his ex, I was sure of it. I was afraid she might make a violent attempt at me. Maybe, one day, she would stand in front of my door with a knife in her hand. John didn't care. I bought a new mailbox.

*   *   *

Over the following weeks, John got more and more aggressive toward me. I felt his emotional ups and downs as if they were my own. My high sensitivity and intuitive abilities tortured me day in and day out.

"What is going on with you? You are becoming increasingly aggressive, your energy toward me has changed, and you are withdrawing from me. Tell me, what is going on?"

I asked him, trying to figure out what was happening.

"You know the saying the grass is always greener on the other side of the river?"

"Yes. What does that have to do with us?"

Then it dawned on me. He was going back and forth because wherever he stood, the woman on the other side was more attractive to him. He was about to go back to his ex-girlfriend -again.

"You know that the business has been quite tough for me and my start-ups," he continued.

He switched the topic. He didn't want to continue explaining himself.

"Uhm . . . Yes. And what? The business has always been like that. You are always trying to figure out what could happen. As long as you have a strategy and a plan and execute it properly, everything will work out. And even methods and techniques can fail. You may need to talk with your start-ups."

"You want to advise and recommend what I should do?" He smirked.

I realized the truth underneath his question. I was surprised. He was a brilliant, successful, intelligent lawyer but felt insecure because of my massive management and business background, which he missed. He was a lawyer and less of an entrepreneur or manager. His lack of self-esteem led to his aggression against me - bad news. I was willing to speak about almost everything. And I can't stand or respect men who try to compensate for their insecurity at my expense and by being competitive and aggressive toward me.

"After almost a year working with your start-ups, I can tell you much about them. Who is working hard, and who doesn't? Some of them don't listen to me but think they have better ideas regarding marketing and sales. Some don't get it because they are not smart enough. They are doing their own thing despite being told differently. What will happen if they fail to follow the strategy execution we agreed upon? They take advantage of you, being convinced you will continue to be their cash cow, and investing no matter what they do,"

"Interesting. What should I do? What would you recommend if you were in my shoes?" His voice had some derisive tone underneath.

"There is a saying: no money, no honey. Giving them an ultimatum about executing plans with deadlines and key performance indicators would be best. Otherwise, you stop transferring money. What will your investors do if they realize no return on investment? They will hold you accountable for those investments, not them. If there is no honey and no results, there won't be any money soon. And you know that. The start-ups do not. They behave like kids in play school."

John looked at me blankly.

"Listen. I want to help you because you asked me to support those start-up kids. Why don't you reduce the number of projects? You don't need due diligence for every project people ask you to do. You need to balance your resources, personally and professionally."

"I haven't heard these recommendations before," he responded arrogantly.

"Why don't you go back and focus on your law firm? You have been and will always be successful in that area. These start-up kids are too risky to build your life on and make a living. It would help to let this go because it's not worth it. You won't become a start-up millionaire overnight or in three months. That's an illusion. Money doesn't grow on trees. What if the investors stop investing?"

"No, all this law nonsense is a boring game. I see myself and my future in the investment sector. I want to make money in the new world of the internet and e-commerce."

"Great, but it's a dream with a small chance to succeed with these startups."

"You don't know. You have never tried it by yourself!"

I gave up. I shook my head, stood up, and returned to my desk.

*   *   *

Two weeks later, I organized an art exhibition in our new offices to invite our new and old clients for a meet and greet. I had a second business running as an art dealer for Native American art. I had brought twenty art pieces—drawings, oil on canvas, collages, and sand painting—from Santa Fe, New Mexico, to Germany. I curated this exhibition at the American House and Chamber in Munich under the patronage of the General Consulate of the American Embassy and several corporate sponsors. With over five hundred people attending the opening show and high media coverage in print and TV, it was a great success.

It was an exhibition of contemporary Native American art that people in Germany hadn't seen before. I still held several art pieces that had not been sold during the exhibition and decided to hang them in our shared offices.

Many clients and friends came to see the artwork. The evening started great, and everyone enjoyed walking around with a drink and mingling with friends, clients, or new people arriving. Unfortunately, Jessica and her jellyfish husband showed up, too. John and Jessica hadn't seen each other for quite a while, but they seemed happy to meet again. After the official part of the speeches and the art tour I gave was over, everyone mingled, chatted, and drank. John flirted with Jessica, and she gave him her undivided attention. It hurt, but I didn't want to make a scene again. Time went by quickly while I talked with guests and drank wine. I got tired and started to look for John. He had disappeared.

"Where is John?" I asked Ed.

"I don't know, maybe in his office."

Then it dawned on me. Jessica wasn't there either, but her husband was still at the party. About an hour later, John and Jessica returned to the room and mingled with all the others again. John had a giddy grin and a certain glance in his eyes, which I was very familiar with. For sure, both had had fun together. Anger crawled up my throat. I didn't say anything when they came in, pretending not to have seen them or know anything.

But this time, and for the first time, I initiated a fight with John. I was out of rage and felt utterly helpless. It was embarrassing for both of us to fight in front of our colleagues and some friends who stayed a little longer.

I left the party and abandoned him the same night.

As expected, he had nothing better to do than return to his ex-girlfriend that night again. I hated him for doing that. He was taking advantage of two women loving him and a third one he on-and-off had sex with.

What I loved about him in the beginning had become my nightmare. Watching him flirt with everyone—men or women—in our shared office hurt terribly. I could hardly concentrate on my projects and clients.

I called my sister when I got home. She always had good advice.

"I have left him again. I can't help it, but this man drives me crazy."

"Great idea. I told you so, and I am glad you made the final decision."

When she said the two words, "final decision," I cried. I didn't want it to end, but I couldn't live like this any longer.

"Words don't count as long as no actions are following. Please don't be so stupid and believe everything John says. He is a lawyer trained not to tell the truth to defend his client in front of the court. But you are brilliant, as well. Don't let him pull your chain," she reminded me.

"I know, I know. I don't let John get away with everything he is telling me. That's why we have been fighting more and more often. He wants to be right all the time, no matter what. He twists and bends the truth just as he wants it to."

"What do you mean, exactly?"

"He likes it to attack me verbally out of nowhere. He bullies me. He claims that I am mean or arrogant or whatever to humiliate me. He can't prove it, though. And I start to defend myself. He doesn't accept it. In the rare cases I have defeated him, he stood up and left the room or even my apartment. Our fights are so painful. That's not love. I often think that he has a sadistic character trait or he is a psychopath."

"So, it's great that you left him. You don't deserve such a jerk on your side. Listen, I am tired, and I have a tough day tomorrow. Let's speak over the weekend. I will call you on Sunday."

I was sad. I wanted to continue talking with her till every thought and emotion was on the table, but she didn't like to. That was okay.

I couldn't understand why someone like John could speak in a way that touched my heart so many times, and a minute later, his words and actions were the opposite. Sticking to my decision was easy, though I missed him terribly. I soaked my pain in a bottle of red wine that night and every night that followed.

*　*　*

I visited our shared office for the first time after ten days. I didn't want to see John. Every day, I called my assistant Robbie for an update on the projects he mostly managed. He did a great job, which allowed me to work from home.

On Sunday afternoon, I decided to go into the office and check the mail that had come in the last few days. Thank God, nobody was there. I felt weird. The Native American artwork was still hanging on the walls, staring at me. I loved every piece because it was exclusive and hard to find. The artists carefully selected every work based on a concept I had created: "From the Outside Looking In," which was the exhibition's title and catalog.

It took me several months in Santa Fe to collect artworks from five different tribes and artistic styles. The Native Americans featured in the artwork seemed to be looking at me, saying, "Where have you been?".
I smiled at them. The art pieces and I had become well-known and

trusted friends, and I was happy to see them again. It was a quiet and peaceful Sunday afternoon in the office. I could hardly remember how I felt that party night while fighting with John.

I sat at my desk, an oval conference table made from bright enamel in the specific color of vermilion. I loved this unusual table with its shining surface. Together with several sideboards made from dark gray iron, the table gave my office a creative look. In addition, my office space was the only one that had walls made of glass. So, everybody could see but not hear me and vice versa. I called it an aquarium because people still determine who is watching whom. A colossal window from top to bottom opened the space behind my chair, bringing light and a view of green trees into it.

I checked the mail piled on my desk, did the accounting, and answered some emails when I heard someone knocking on the glass door. I was John standing there. I got frightened at first and had to catch my breath. I didn't expect him to come here on a Sunday, and I didn't hear or see him walk into the office through the main door. John looked at me and made some pantomimic gestures to enter my aquarium.

"Can I come in?"

I glanced at him, nodded, and stopped working on my laptop.

"I am glad that I found you here." He took one of the visitor's chairs from the other side of the table, sat right next to me, looked into my eyes, and grabbed my hands.

"I want you to marry me."

"What?" I withdrew my hands. I took a deep breath.

"What? Is this a proposal?"

"Yes. I am unprepared for that, but I have thought about us for the last ten days. There is no one more important in my life than you. No one. Please become my wife. Would you marry me?"

I was speechless. I felt nothing. I was in shock.

"Why should I believe you now?"

"Because I love you and want to be with you."

"I wouldn't flirt or have sex with someone else when my significant other stands beside me or in the next room, as you have done so many times. While we were together, you also had sex with your ex-girlfriend and with Jessica, too. That's disgusting. I don't trust you at all."

I got upset again. I couldn't help it. Here sat the man I loved, proposing to me, and I was fighting for my values and sanity. He had hurt me too often.

"Are you going to marry me?"

He didn't want to address what I was saying. He looked at me and grabbed my hands again. He wasn't afraid at all and didn't give up.

"Yes and no. I don't know. Give me twenty-four hours to think about it. Let's meet for dinner tomorrow night, and I will let you know."

"I understand. Maybe I'm moving too fast. Let's meet at our favorite Italian restaurant tomorrow night. I am looking forward to seeing you. Don't overthink the past. Just make the right decision." He smiled.

Then he went back to his apartment and his old girlfriend. Were they separated, meanwhile? I had no idea. Did she know what he had just asked me? Surely not.

I could not believe what had just happened. I had grown tired of our fights and John's intent to reconcile, but no action followed. On the other hand, why should he ask me to marry him after all our terrible fights? There was no need for him to do that. John had made a final and significant decision. I was sure.

*   *   *

"Yes, I will marry you."

The first thing I said to him after we had ordered a glass of wine in our Italian restaurant. I didn't know why, but I said yes. It was like some other person spoke through me. It felt right, but not even a glimpse of a joyful feeling came with it. John was excited. He moved his chair to sit beside me, kissing and holding me in his arms.

"She said yes! We will get married!"

John cheered out loud into the restaurant so everybody could hear it. The entire restaurant applauded, and he ordered a bottle of champagne to celebrate our engagement.

Finally, it seemed we had overcome our challenges and were together. But something was holding me back from the deep feeling of joy that I knew very well from my first marriage. It felt like being on stage acting in a theater play. I didn't tell him about how I felt inside.

The next day, John officially announced our engagement to our colleagues and his partners in the law office. Ed had been asked to be his best man. He joyfully agreed. He was happy for both of us. Ed knew how much I had suffered while John went back and forth for the previous nine months. That morning, John packed his car with shirts, trousers, and suits to move into my home again, for the third time, or was it the fourth time? I wasn't sure whether his former girlfriend knew that things had changed dramatically for her. She knew he had moved back again to me and into my place, but he still kept some of his clothes in their apartment.

The telephone terror resumed. The caller's ID was suppressed whenever these scary calls came in. I picked up the phone. There was no voice, but somebody made strange noises, like a high-pitched sound that hurt my ears. I got anxious after a while. I felt threatened. Again, John denied it could be his ex-girlfriend's attempt to scare me. I told him that I would not pick up the phone in the future when I wouldn't see an ID. One day, the phone rang. Somebody with a Munich number called me. I picked up the phone, and there again was the high-pitched sound. I hung up.

My heart was pounding. A few minutes later, after I had calmed down, I got furious. I took my phone and dialed the number I had seen on the phone screen. It took several ringtones until a woman answered my call. It wasn't her.

"I want to speak with the person who just called my number. Was it you or somebody else from your office?" I harshly reacted after she introduced herself.

"I'm sorry, but I didn't call you. We are a law office, and I am the assistant to the managing director. My assistant colleague sits across from me and just left for lunch. I pick up her phone while she is out. Can I leave her a message?"

It was clear and definite that John's ex-girlfriend was the telephone terrorist. I knew that she was working at this law office. Finally, I had proof.

"Yes, you can. Would you tell this bitch - I have never met or spoken to in person - to stop chasing me with her anonymous calls, trying to scare me. She is my boyfriend's ex-girlfriend. My name is Gabby, and she has been doing this daily for years. I am fed up. I have installed a recorder on my phone. If she calls me again, I will call the police and your boss, your law firm's managing director, to ensure she gets fired. I am furious about her sick behavior."

"How do you know it was her?" the assistant replied calmly. She thought she was brilliant, trying to defend her colleague. I rolled my eyes.

"Lady, I simply redialed the number she called me from, and you picked up. She should have remembered to deactivate the ID like she has done over the last two years. It's a big mistake, lady. I will make sure the police catch her."

I hung up and told John what I had figured out. He couldn't believe it. Indeed, in the following weeks, the telephone terror stopped. I am sure her colleague noted my call in the law office, telling her what would happen if she didn't stop. Finally, my phone became silent after so many years of telephone terror. I was relieved.

* * *

John and I flew to Los Angeles at the end of July. We planned to spend a week in Malibu, taking some days off. I had to get out of the office and needed some fresh ocean breeze. He had some business to care for, and I wanted to prepare for our wedding. We stayed at the same hotel next to the

Malibu Pier during the last New Year's Eve visit. I enjoyed the sun and the sound of my beloved Pacific Ocean.

I should have known better. A day after our arrival, we ate lunch at a great Italian restaurant at the Malibu Court. John started to fight again. He began to accuse me out of the blue. I was looking at the menu, trying to decide what to eat. My stomach had become very sensitive during the last two years, reacting with cramps to almost anything I was eating. Thus, I had become very picky about what I ordered.

"Can't you order what is on the menu, like everybody else? You always want something special. Do you think you are that special?"

John looked at me, quite embarrassed.

One thing I like about any restaurant in the States is that you can order unique dishes of what you like and how you want them to be cooked, and nobody complains. Instead, they are happy to serve you the food as you would like it. He didn't know that compared to Germany, excellent customer service is a central part of the US culture.

"What? Are you starting to fight about the food I am ordering? What is wrong with you?"

"I don't like it when people think they can command waiters."

"You are nuts! It's their job to bring the food I like to eat. That's what I pay for and why they get a tip. Please stop attacking me. I want to enjoy being here. That's my special sweet spot of the universe."

We were fighting again. I couldn't believe it. After we had eaten, John went back to the hotel. I took a walk on the beach by myself. I needed to get his negative energy out of my body and mind. I love sitting on the beach, looking at the endless horizon, and watching the pelicans. I was sad and angry at the same time. The dolphins came to swim by, which filled my heart with joy. When I returned to the hotel, the sun went down with a beautiful sunset.

He was sitting at the desk with his laptop and working. His mood seemed to have improved.

"Come on, let's go to the restaurant on the beach, have a sundowner and a bite to eat."

He had pulled himself together, and we had a great evening. The next day was challenging again. I had no idea why he had such mood swings. I assumed that it had something to do with the business. He didn't want to talk about it when I asked him. However, I know much about behavioral patterns, language, and body language. He barely spoke to me when we ate dinner the following evening.

"Let's speak about our wedding," I suggested, hoping to lighten his mood.

"I have more important things to do. Can't you see that?" he harshly replied.

"Aha…I understand. So, let's discuss a date and who we will invite. That would be enough information for me to start planning, and you don't have to bother."

"No, I have too many things to do in the next few months. I can't even think about a wedding. I don't have the time."

"Okay, what about next year?"

"I told you. I am still determining what's going to happen with the business. I cannot make any plans."

"So, no wedding this year nor next year?"

He didn't reply, and I realized our connection was broken again. I had no idea why, but we had to start all over again.

When I woke up the following day, he was already working at his computer.

"What is going on? Is everything okay?" I asked John.

He didn't reply.

"What are we going to do today?"

John looked up briefly but didn't respond. He focused on his laptop. I went into the bathroom, brushed my teeth, and showered. The entire area around my heart started to hurt again. It was a burning pain, like someone had put a knife into my heart chakra and moved it around. Again. My body ached. I felt I was at his mercy to heal that pain and realized he wouldn't.

I woke up from my dream—finally. He would never commit—never. And it didn't matter whether he couldn't or wouldn't. It was a sudden insight like a lightbulb. I yearned to be free from this pain, from him. I wanted to be free in every way—emotionally and mentally. What happened between us over almost two years was not the life I wanted or wished for. No one would.

I dressed, put on makeup, and packed my suitcase. I didn't say a word. I grabbed my jean jacket and walked to the door with my luggage and purse. John looked up for the first time.

"What are you doing?"

He asked as if he had not realized that I had been packing my luggage for the last thirty minutes.

"I'm leaving."

"Where are you going?" He still was looking at the screen of his laptop. "Are you going to the beach?"

"No, I am leaving you and everything that happened between us. I am fed up with your fights, your accusations, your neglecting me and our wedding, and your disrespectful behavior. Everything. I don't deserve to be treated like that. Remember, you asked me to marry you, not the other way around. You don't deserve a woman like me. You have to learn a lot about love and commitment."

"You don't have a car."

"Well, that is not a problem. There is a car rental station right across the street. I will go there and get a car. It's not my first time renting a car, and I will drive alone. Have you forgotten who I am, who you are dealing with? I am an independent woman and successful entrepreneur, and I have always lived and can easily live without you."

I shook my head, grabbed my suitcase, and left our hotel room.

"Wait, are you leaving *me*?"

It dawned on him what was going to happen.

"Yes!"

He jumped up from his chair.

"I will accompany you to the rental car station."

"Why? It won't make a difference. I can handle it on my own. I am not your former, childlike ex-girlfriend. I am grown up."

Nonetheless, he walked me to the rental station. I rented a nice white Mustang convertible for two weeks, knowing our flight back to Munich would leave in three days. I would have to change the flight. John took my suitcase and put it in the trunk.

"Where are you going?"

"I don't know yet. Just cruising." I opened the convertible top.

"When are you coming back?"

I didn't and couldn't answer. I had no plan or idea what to do or where to go next. But I intuitively knew that I had to leave him. This was it. I crashed the wedding plans. I felt devastated, but getting out of his dark energy and destructive behavior was the only way to save my life.

I jumped into my new white Mustang and started the engine.

"Enjoy Malibu," I smiled and drove off.

I saw his surprised expression in the rearview mirror and felt relieved for the first time in almost two years. I knew I had to escape from these emotional ups and downs; it felt like I was burning in hell. Cruising along the Pacific Coast Highway, the blue sky and Pacific Ocean to the left, and desert hills with beautiful mansions and villas to the right, breathing fresh air soothed me and helped to clear my mind. After a while, I regained my inner balance and thought about what I could do in the next few weeks. It was August, and many people were surfing and celebrating summer break.

I called my German friend Andrea to meet for lunch. She lived in Los Angeles for over twenty years, successfully worked as a film producer, and married an American architect. She was happily surprised that I was in town.

We met for lunch in Silver Lake near her office. I told her the entire story and what had happened.

"Sweetheart, I feel so sorry for you. Why don't you drive north to the Esalen Institute in Big Sur, about six hours along the PCH, the Pacific Coast Highway? It's a beautiful drive. It's a retreat and the perfect place for you right now. It's built on cliffs over the Pacific Ocean."

"Sounds like the perfect trip and place for me right now."

"They have pools with natural spring water to soak in, organic food grown right there, and lovely wooden cabins to stay in overnight. To stay there, you must attend one of their workshops on spirituality and creativity. You can learn how to meditate, join spiritual classes, dance, paint, or even work there."

Andrea knows me very well. She always has a great idea of how to overcome obstacles and challenges. We met four years earlier at one of her acting workshops in Hollywood, which she was running in addition to her film production company. I wanted to learn complex acting craft because I loved stepping into different roles; even for my business, it was helpful. Andrea and I have become trusted friends since then.

I checked online on the Esalen website whether workshops would be available as of the next day or the day after, hoping it might be a place to stay for a while. I was lucky. Esalen offered a five-day meditation workshop about to start two days later, and seats were available. I booked it immediately, spent one night at Andrea's place, and started my new adventure the following day, driving up north of California along the beautiful Pacific Ocean. In Santa Barbara, I stopped for a quick break, got gas, a snack, water, and continued driving.

Looking at the blue Pacific Ocean while driving along the coast was soothing—a dream had come true. Once in a while, I stopped the car and walked to the cliff, listening to the waves crashing on the shore. I wanted to take nature all in. I arrived at Big Sur and checked in at the Esalen Institute in the evening.

The first week, I shared a small wooden cabin with another woman, Beth, who came from Canada and also needed a break.

During the second week, the entire cabin was all mine. I loved it. I didn't speak to anyone for two weeks except to introduce myself at the beginning of the meditation class and when asking for food during the meal breaks.

Every morning, during every break and evening, I walked over to a lonesome old, dark-green bench placed under an old pine tree, right on the edge of one cliff facing the entire ocean.

I sat down, doing nothing but watching and listening to the rolling waves coming in, softly moving the sea surface up and down. I couldn't see them when they broke offshore, but I could hear them, a silent sound that calmed my mind over time. My chaotic inner thoughts, inner movie scenes, and memories of hurtful emotions from the previous two years slowly lessened.

I spent four weeks in California in total. It was the best decision I could have made in caring for myself for the first time in years. It was the end of August when I flew back to Munich. I had been out of the office the entire time, and I planned to check in with my assistant Robbie quickly, do my emails, meet with my clients, friends, and family for one week, and then return to California. I had already booked a flight to Los Angeles for the end of the following week. There was not much to do because everybody had been on vacation in Europe in August.

I wanted to spend as little time as possible in the office. I was nervous when I drove up there, but I had to go in. I realized that I still felt vulnerable about what had happened.

When I opened the main door and stepped into the office, John and Ed walked straight toward me. I did not expect to see them, nor did they expect me to open the door and enter. Both stopped instantly and looked at me in awe. I stopped, too. I was shocked. I couldn't go one step further. John gazed at me, speechless, shocked as well. Ed was the first to find his voice.

"Hi, Gabby. It's good to see you again. Where have you been the last four weeks?" He looked at me joyfully, then at John, then at me again.

"You guys talk—now!" Ed commanded with a severe face, pushing John and me into my aquarium-like glass office. He turned around to check who else was in the vast office space and immediately ordered them to leave for lunch. Ed was such a great character. I was grateful that he did that. Everyone grabbed their stuff and rushed to leave, passing my office and waving at me.

"I heard that you had locked yourself in a monastery."

"Yes and no, not really. It was a retreat, and I was in silence. Who told you that?"

"I heard Robbie speaking with you. After your call, I asked him where you were."

"How long did you stay in the hotel in Malibu? Did you enjoy your remaining days?"

"No, I left Los Angeles the day you left with your white Mustang. I couldn't stay there one more day. Although, when I looked out the window in the plane while we flew over Malibu, I deeply regretted leaving too fast," he said. "I wondered where you were that evening."

"Why did you move out of my apartment?"

John looked at me as if he didn't understand the question.

"It didn't cross your mind to stay in the apartment, check on me while I was in the US, and wait for me to return? You know my phone number. I was your fiancée…and would have been if you had cared for me while I was in the States."

"Well, yes…you are right." John stumbled.

"What was the first thing you did when returning to Germany? You moved in again with your ex-girlfriend! Didn't you?"

He looked at me with wide eyes.

"Well then, why did you return to your ex-girlfriend right after returning to Germany? If it had been so difficult to live in my apartment while I was in the States, you could have checked into a hotel to pause and think about our relationship and what you really want. You should not have returned to her, but you could have spoken to me first about why I abandoned you in Malibu. We were engaged. Does it always have to be your way or highway?"

John stared at me, realizing that his view of a relationship wasn't compatible with the reality of a commitment. I had counted on him, which was my mistake. I felt silly.

"You didn't call me or check whether I was okay in the US. Does a marriage commitment mean nothing to you? For sure, it means a lot to me. This commitment is a decision that doesn't happen out of nowhere, like deciding what to have for dinner. It's inclusive, in good times and in bad times. You are a bastard!"

Again, I got angry the minute I saw him. I wanted to slap him in the face.

"Anyhow, our relationship has come to an end. I have booked a flight back to the States next Friday. I will stay in San Francisco for a few days and then drive to Los Angeles for another three weeks. I have also decided to terminate my rental agreement for your office space. I will move my office back to Munich when I return at the end of September. I will give you the termination letter tomorrow."

From that moment, John treated me like he was carrying a raw egg. He was caring, extremely respectful, and affectionate, as if he saw me for the first time. I didn't show appreciation other than being as friendly as I usually treat my clients. I kept my broken heart locked and the key hidden in a box.

"Can I drive you to the airport?" John asked me the day before I left.

"Yes, you can."

He helped me check in my luggage for my flight to San Francisco. He hugged me goodbye and watched me until I had passed the passport control and security check. I turned around. Should I have stayed? No, it was the right thing to do. I shook my head but felt like an addict to this man.

*　　*　　*

After I arrived in San Francisco, I drove to a friend's place I had met during the meditation workshop at the Esalen Institute in Big Sur. Her name was Karen, and she was an artist and sculpting teacher. She was a pretty woman in her fifties with long, blonde hair and dressed like a hippie. She owned a beautiful place in the wealthy residential area of San Francisco near the Pacific Coast.

My room and separate bathroom were beautifully furnished. I enjoyed staying there and spending time in her artists' studio.

Every day, John texted, called, or sent pictures of Munich. He wanted to reconnect, seduce me to come back again. He sent emails with the most beautiful love letters I had ever read, but they didn't touch me in my heart. I didn't feel anything any longer. And I couldn't care less from the other end of planet Earth, five thousand miles away. I had experienced his narcissistic games so many times and didn't want to go through hell again.

Then, one morning, after I woke up, brushed my teeth, and showered, I switched on my mobile phone. I couldn't believe what John wrote:

"Turn on the TV when you read this. The Third World War has begun…"

It was the day in 2001 that had stopped the world from turning: 9/11. That was the last message I received from him for a week, at least.

"Karen, please turn on the TV. Right now, there is something terrible going on in the world."

She turned on the TV, and we were in shock, looking at the videos of the planes crashing into the Twin Towers in New York City, the Pentagon, and nearby San Francisco. We were frozen. I cried, looking at the horrifying pictures. I was reminded of my stay in Tehran, the same month twenty-three years earlier.

"This terrorist attack is not a normal one. That's a jihad."

"What is a jihad?" Karen asked.

"The motives behind the attack are religious. Fanatic Islamic terrorists want to destroy anything representing Western culture, lifestyle, and symbols connected with the Jewish or Christian religion. One well-known symbol of Western culture is the Twin Towers in NYC. The USA and their people are the symbolic representation of what they hate."

"How do you know? We don't know yet who were the insane people who did this. You are very convinced."

"I can't tell for sure. It's my instinct. I might be wrong, but I don't think so. Once, I was trapped in a civil war where exactly that happened: sudden terrorist attacks on the symbols of anything representing the Western world and culture, especially from the United States. Secondly, I was on a business trip to Cairo, Egypt, three months ago with my former fiancé. Because it was so hot in the city, I spent one afternoon in the hotel room with AC. I turned on the TV, and a report about so-called terrorist camps in Egypt caught my interest."

"No way...they publicly named a training camp for young men as terrorist camps?"

"Yes, that was the official name for the camps in the TV report, where young Islamists were trained to kill so-called evil. I don't remember the place of the camp. Evil, from their perspective, is everything and everyone from Western civilization. The attacks go against Christians, Jews, and foremost against the people from the USA. I was horrified watching this report. Yet, I hadn't seen anything like that in the German or US news before. It seemed nobody knew, or journalists didn't want to publish that terrifying information. Now, I know why I am scared."

Karen and I sat in front of the TV, watching the latest news all day. Everyone was on their toes about whether another attack would happen.

My mobile phone and every landline were shut off whenever I tried to call John or my sister. I didn't receive calls either. I wasn't even able to send an email to Germany. The entire nation had been cut off from any communication with foreign countries. A symbolic iron wall was built around the continent because nobody could fly out or into the United States for a week. I drove to Los Angeles three days later to meet my friend Andrea and others.

* * *

The Pacific Coast Highway, with the ocean view, looked as beautiful as always, but it wasn't the same anymore. Every car that passed had the American flag stuck to the window. Everyone felt the urge to show unity, grief, and compassion for the victims of this terror attack. I bought a flag, too, and put it on my car window. I felt even more connected to the people in the US because I knew what it felt like when terrorists attack out of nowhere.

The following two weeks in Los Angeles were quite strange. The emotional aftermath of the terrorist attacks was like heavy clouds over the city and the ocean, creating a certain silence and stillness. Everyone was traumatized and in fear. Was there another terror attack planned? If so, when would it happen, and where? Security and police forces in LA could be seen everywhere, making me feel better and safer. They were the reminder of what had just happened in NYC, Washington, and nearby San Francisco.

When communication was turned on again, John called me every day until I boarded the airplane back to Munich. He was devastated and had the urge to rescue me again. He couldn't because there were no flights left for LAX.

*   *   *

John and I talked a lot about his start-up business. He told me he needed money on short-term notice because the banks who had given him loans wanted their money back. He needed 45,000 euros. He didn't ask me to help him, but I wanted to. I saw how hard he had worked for the last two years, and I knew how difficult it was and how much money was needed to launch a company. I signed a check for 20,000 euros on my company's behalf and gave him a private loan of another 25,000 euros. He signed the two contracts and promised to pay back the money within the next two weeks. It didn't occur to me that he would betray me. Although he was a terrible man for a romantic relationship, I trusted his words as a businessman. He had been a highly credited lawyer but was a wolf in sheepskin. I was the naïve sheep, mixing business with my private emotions—a big mistake.

As before, we came together again, but after forty-eight hours, we started to fight again. I got jealous when I discovered John had already begun another affair with his assistant while still living together with his ex-girlfriend and while I was in Los Angeles. He was still the narcissistic womanizer with no ethics or values I had met two years ago. He hadn't learned anything at all, but neither had I. My hurt feelings from the past had crawled back.

I moved out of the office two months later. It was painful; I had no idea why. I should have been happy, but it made me sad. My time with John was very intense, both good and bad. His colleagues and partners had become my peers, my family of choice. I liked them a lot, and I missed them. I had to leave them, too. Separation is painful in many directions, although I had decided it on my own.

At the beginning of 2002, the stock market of highly valued internet companies crashed. I had invested in the new market and lost all my savings, all of them. Still, there was the money I had given to John. He had promised to pay it back within two weeks. But four months had passed, and I hadn't seen a dime. I called him and emailed him. He had no response other than, "The check is in the mail, " and he lied every time I asked. Every time, he lied. I got angry about his nasty and disrespectful behavior, trying to get away with it. He didn't even attempt to explain the delay or ask for rescheduling. He hoped that I would give up one day. He had no idea how bull-headed I could become to find justice, especially when someone tried to betray me.

After another two months of talking with friends about how to get my money back, someone recommended speaking with Peter, a well-respected insolvency trustee. I wondered why I should talk to such an expert, but after ten minutes of speaking with him, I knew precisely why.

"You know, there is a law that your company as a creditor can file bankruptcy for his company at the local district court. This way, you can get back part of the money that you lent him."

"Really? What do you mean?"

"It's not a nice thing to do, especially not among friends, but I guess you are no longer friends. He hasn't treated you appropriately. He should be grateful that you gave him so much money and saved his ass from insolvency and banks who want their money back."

"I am anxious that I won't see any money at all. John owes even higher amounts of money to several banks. They will be served first in case of his bankruptcy."

"What I mean is that you should go to him and tell him that if he is unwilling to pay back his debt to your company, you will file bankruptcy for his company. If you don't want to be that tough, you can ask him to sign a legal document that is as good as a court's decision. Thus, you don't need to file a lawsuit and go to court. This document is like a verdict, which means if he doesn't pay back within the time you demand, you can go to the police with the document, and they will arrest him. He will go to jail. He knows the rules; he is a lawyer."

"Oh wow...that scares me a lot. How are we going to do that? I can't go there by myself and threaten him. Besides, they won't let me walk into the office. But they don't know you. They will open the door for you. Would you come with me and speak to him?"

"No problem. That's my daily job. When is best to go there, in the morning or late afternoon? Every office has its rhythm. "

"Let's meet there on Wednesday next week at 11:00 a.m. They usually start later and stay longer."

We drove to the office building with its four stories on Wednesday morning. I had worked there for two years. To not be seen, I parked my car under a tree in the far back of the building. We walked through the janitor's side door into the building and took the stairs to the second floor. Sometime before, I was surprised to hear from Ed that they couldn't afford the vast office space after I had terminated the rental agreement. Ed had also moved out and rented a much smaller office in the same building. John's team had also moved into another office but in the same building.

The main office door was a big wooden one that opened outside to the hall. It was surrounded by two small windows from bottom to top. When Peter rang the doorbell, he stood right before the left window to be seen. I was hiding behind the wooden door. The assistant, John's new love affair, opened a minute later and looked at Peter. She couldn't see me.

"How can I help you?"

"My name is Peter. I want to speak with John on an urgent matter."

"He is not here. He is in court. Why don't you come back at 2:00 p.m.?"

In this second, it dawned on me that John would never let him in because of urgent matters. He would sense that Peter's visit would have something to do with his financial problems, which would mean more trouble.

I grabbed the doorknob, fully opened the door with one swing, and walked in without looking at her. Peter followed me right away. She glanced at me in surprise, maybe in shock, but couldn't stop me. Gray carpets, white walls, and gray furniture were seen in several offices and a conference room. I stopped and looked at her condescendingly.

"I am sure one of John's partners is here. We can also talk to them. My company gave his company money, not John personally. You know that, too, because you are the assistant and know all the numbers. You guys are responsible for paying back the debt, and you know it. We are happy to talk to either one of his partners. I don't need John to get my money back."

"Okay. I will call John. Have a seat in the conference room. I will let the others know that you are here."

I was relieved that we managed to get in. Otherwise, it would have been challenging to come back again, and John would have prevented us from getting in again. I wanted to stay until we had negotiated a solution.

Peter and I were sitting in the conference room for at least twenty minutes without anybody coming in. Finally, one of his partners arrived to tell us they wanted to wait until John returned. They had already called him, telling him I was sitting in the conference room with another man. But they had yet to learn who Peter was and why he accompanied me.

"This could take another two hours; John just told us." Thomas, one of John's business partners, told me.

"We will wait," Peter replied, friendly.

"So, what do you want, Gabby?"

"What do you assume, Thomas? Don't you think I have better things to do than coffee with you guys? Your company owes me money, and I want it back—now."

Peter started the negotiation: "I am Peter, and I act as an insolvency administrator in Gabby's name. As John's business partner, you know that Gabby's company gave your company 20,000 euros as a credit and another 25,000 euros to John personally. That was a year ago. John had signed a credit agreement and committed to pay it back within two weeks. Until today, neither she nor her company has seen any money despite several letters, calls, and emails with false promises. Enough is enough."

"Yes, we know. We don't have the money. She has to wait." Thomas replied.

"No, she doesn't have to wait and won't wait any longer. You must give her the money in cash today."

"We don't have that much money in our safe," Thomas answered.

"Then go to your bank, get the money in cash, and come back. We will wait here."

"I have to speak with John first because he has to confirm the amount. The bank would only give us the money with his signature. He will be here in about twenty minutes. We just called him."

"Okay, we will wait."

I was surprised and grateful for how tough and stern Peter could speak. He was not the guy somebody dared to fool. He knew what he was doing. Thomas left and kept the door open. Sitting at the end of the conference table, I saw John come in ten minutes later. He didn't stop to greet us but passed the conference room without looking at the open door and walked straight into his office with a grim face.

Another ten minutes later, Thomas came back to us.

"We can't get the money from the bank. The amount needs to be lowered. We will have to collect it, which will take around four weeks. Gabby, we will give you back the full amount in four weeks."

"No, don't even think about it. We don't believe you at all. It has to be done now," Peter replied without waiting for my response. "Do you know what we will do if you don't pay her back the money in the next two hours?" he continued.

"No, what could you do? Haha. You can't do anything. Gabby must wait!" Thomas's arrogant response and laughter were unbearable.

"I thought you guys were lawyers. You need to learn how to satisfy your creditors! It's embarrassing."

"What else will you do? Do you want to threaten us with a gun?" Thomas replied with a grin on his face. He felt secure and safe. His dirty smile would be stuck in his throat within a minute. I knew it, and that felt good. There was no mercy and no empathy for those criminals. I had gained my power back.

"Well, your smile will disappear pretty soon! We will go to the local district court five minutes away and file your company bankruptcy today because you can't pay back your debts. We will do that right now because I am a certified liquidator, and we don't hesitate to walk to the court now."

Peter's voice had become harsh. He stood up immediately and looked at me to stand up as well. I did.

"No, no . . . wait a moment. You can't do that. Please wait. I will speak with John again. Maybe he'll find another way."

Thomas seemed shocked. He would have lost his job and professional existence within ten minutes.

"The only other option Gabby would accept is a signed financial replacement form that is as good as a verdict. If you sign the document here, she will give you another week to transfer the money to her company's bank account. What will happen if you don't pay your debt that day? Do you know? Let me tell you: one of you will go to jail. Immediately, because we will call the police and they will arrest one of you. For sure, there is no exception. Gabby's patience is exhausted; no mercy is left. One of you will go into prison."

Thomas's face went pale. He rushed out of the room. Five minutes later, he came back.

"We accept, but we need four weeks, please. Please write June 30 as the date. We won't have the money earlier," he begged. They seemed to have understood that their game was over.

I looked at Thomas and felt terrible. I was sad that our friendship had ended so dramatically. Who would have ever expected that? But I had to do what I had to do.

Peter filled out the document, including the amount and payback time, and had me sign it. Thomas then took the document and walked over into John's office. Peter and I sat back again. He looked at me, nodded, and smiled. One minute later, Thomas came in with the signed document. I took the record, and Peter and I left the office.

John didn't show up in person at all. He didn't have the guts to look me in the eyes and negotiate with me directly. I had lost literally five pounds during these two hours of negotiating. I was exhausted but happy that I would finally get my money back.

I invited Peter for lunch and talked about what had just happened. I admired him for helping me in that challenging situation.

Four weeks later, the money was transferred to my bank account. But I was still waiting for the other 25,000 euros I gave John as a private loan.

The next day, Ed called. He wanted to see me for lunch immediately. The last time I saw him was when I moved out of the shared office a year ago. The next day, we met for lunch and enjoyed catching up on what had happened since then.

"Gabby, you are my heroine. You did a coup de main two days ago," Ed started with a big smile. "I can't believe it. You tricked John out of his comfort zone by using a simple law that every lawyer knows but he had forgotten. As long as I have known John, no one has dared to do what you did. Ever. You have defeated him and are an equal warrior to him. That was amazing. I am deeply impressed. You are the talk of the town in the legal crowd in Munich. Also, no one in the business building has expected *you* to do what you did and fight against John. *You* are the master, not John."

"How do you know?" I was pretty surprised about his reaction.

"After you left the office two days ago, John came rushing into my office immediately and told me what had happened. He was in total shock. I am proud of you for knocking him off his throne. He deserved it, and nobody could have imagined that you would be the one who would do it."

"Well, that seems my fate. No one expects my power inside and behind my kind attitude. I can wait patiently for a long time—whether business or private. I become a different person when I feel betrayed, when my limits are being exceeded, or when the barrel overflows. It's like a switch inside is flipped. Then, I fight if I want or have to. I am not proud of myself because it's usually not my style. It might be business as usual in your world as a lawyer, but not in mine. John has finally realized that I have never been the victim. I still have a loan open that I gave him. I will find a way to get the remaining money back, too. That's for sure."

"You have all the right to do that. John would have never given you back your money by choice. He is the bad guy; you are the good one. Don't feel guilty."

"By the way, I don't know if you knew that the rent you paid for your shared office with John was not for the tiny space you had taken. You paid the full amount for the entire office space. In other words, you also paid the monthly rent for his office and all start-up companies. He owes you this money as well. He ripped you off all the time, and no one told you - including myself. I should have warned you much earlier. I am so sorry."

"What? Really?" My feelings of guilt disappeared in an instant.

"Why did I fall in love with such a jerk? I was simply in love with him, but he betrayed me and took advantage of me in all significant areas of life: love, relationships, marriage, and money. Everyone knew except me. I was a naïve sheep."

"You are a wolf in sheep's clothes, too. This time, you caught him. You got him. The victory is yours. No one who knows you will ever take advantage of your loving kindness. I was surprised, as well. Everyone in the building is talking about you and your courageous actions. You are the winner. Chapeau, Lady."

"Oh my god. Will anyone ever work with me again in the building? Now, am I the dangerous Iron Lady, or what?"

I had to laugh for the first time. It felt good to talk to him and close this chapter.

"John has yet to consider this law you dug out. Any one of his creditors can do what you announced you would do. I would like to know why the banks he owes money to are not pulling this legal trick. He should be grateful that you didn't go to court directly. Instead, you warned him before."

"It was a little more than a warning, but thank you. I wanted my money, that's all. I assume he has enough money. He can afford to rent offices and pay his employees and himself. I am sure he has a lot of money parked in some anonymous bank accounts in Luxembourg or Switzerland."

"Possible." Ed nodded.

We said goodbye. I was sad that I wouldn't see him often because he was still friends with John.

I filed a lawsuit against John to get the remaining 25,000 euros. Despite winning the case in court, I couldn't get it back. The marshal told me John was unavailable when he approached him to collect my money. Strange. After six months, I decided to stop putting pressure or attention on John, so

I withdrew for a while. I knew him well enough that the minute he would feel "safe" again and not be threatened by his creditors, he would make mistakes. His vanity was his biggest enemy, harming his interests in the business.

* * *

During the new stock market crash, I lost all my savings. My biggest challenge was finding new business and clients because all companies had to cut down their marketing, consulting, and training budgets. Without a job or meaningful work, no people around to talk to, no money, and no loving relationship with a partner, I felt abandoned and again all alone.

I was in agony every day and felt hopeless. I rarely spoke with my friends or my sister about my challenges. Although my sister had listened to my dramatic stories before, she would repeatedly say, "I told you so." This is the last thing you want to hear when you are depressed. Nobody could have helped me, anyhow. It wasn't their fault. Everyone has a busy life and their challenges.

* * *

After a year of grief and sleeplessness, I hit rock bottom. That was it. I had had enough. I decided to pull myself out of the swamp one last time. Nobody else could do it for me but myself.

I started meditating as I had learned it from the Esalen Institute in Big Sur. Every day, I practiced what I learned there about reconnecting with the great spirit. I worked on my résumé as a manager and sent it out to several executive recruiters. One day, I tripped over a master's education program as a business coach and signed up for it. The training lasted two years, and a significant part was learning psychotherapeutic instruments and tools to practice using and healing our own stories and challenges. The training helped me to become grounded and centered again, to clean my inner emotional mess first and before working with people. So I did.

Almost two years later, after the stock market crash, I got hired for an executive position as managing director and country manager for a consumer goods company based in Munich. I got back on my feet and into the game, and my life also turned back to love, connection, and meaning. I felt appreciated again after such a long time of being in darkness.

Despite my financial comeback, I remembered those 25,000 euros John still owed me. Occasionally, I googled his name, checking what he was doing and where he was going. As I assumed, his narcissistic tendencies forced him to publish his activities online on major platforms. He couldn't help it. One day, I saw an ad from a university in Switzerland, where he was announced as a keynote speaker at one of the conferences where investors and start-ups meet and mingle.

I decided to attend the conference. I had no idea what would happen, but I wanted to meet him to remind him of his debts. The week before, I rescheduled my business meetings for that day, took the afternoon off, and drove from Munich to Switzerland. I didn't know why, but I was nervous. While driving the freeway for almost four hours, I remembered everything that had happened during the years when we were together and after that— good and evil. Whatever I remembered, I had to calm myself down because I wanted my money back. He didn't deserve my money as a gift. During all these years, he had never tried to contact me to tell me when he would pay back his debts. Thus, there was no other way than to confront him again.

I arrived at the university fifteen minutes before the conference's official start and several people's presentations. Dressed in a formal, black business suit, I walked into the vast hall expecting to be the only businessperson. My heart was pounding. What should I say? Will he talk to me at all, or would he ignore my showdown?

He saw me immediately and looked straight into my eyes. He was in shock. His eyes were wide open, and his face turned red in a rush. I expected the hall to be full of students. Instead, businesspeople wearing black suits stood around, talking. He seemed to know them well. It was all about investments. I walked to the group where he was standing and said hello.

"Gabby, what a nice surprise. What are you doing here?"

He didn't wait for my answer but immediately introduced me to everyone standing around him. Each was a potential investor from a different company, thinking about putting their money into John's new company. Here we go again. It felt like *Groundhog Day* – the famous movie.

The speech John was about to give was the most important one for his financial future. I had no idea before I arrived, but I came in at the right moment to push my request to get my money back. I wanted the investors to invest in him so that I could get my money back as soon as possible.

The auditorium was quite a big hall with seating for around sixty to one hundred people. The seats were placed on different tiers in half a circle going from top to bottom. The hall looked like a typical old European university arena: gray-white walls, no windows, fluorescent light, uncomfortable brown wooden chairs, a stage, a speaker desk with a microphone, and a white screen wall to project slides.

"We will start in about five minutes. Please have a seat," John told us.

I was the only woman in the lecture hall except for John's girlfriend, the former assistant. As I walked down the aisle in my fabulous business suit, I attracted the attention of all the men in the hall, young and old. They wondered who I was.

I slowly walked down the stairs while everyone was watching me. It was my minute, not his, and I was proud of my courage. I selected the outer seat in the second row close to the speaker's desk. I'm not too fond of being squeezed among so many people. I like aisle seats in general. John took a chair with his girlfriend in the second row, too, but at the opposite end.

The presentations began with a university professor who welcomed the audience. He was surprised to see so many businesspeople in his university. His speech was short, showing several attractive graphics, and I could only partly see what he was talking about. I looked around because I wanted to change my seat to view the screen wall fully. I found one free seat right in the middle of the first row. Sitting there would give me the best idea of the slides presented by John. After the professor had finished his speech, I decided to walk down to this seat.

Twenty minutes later, the presentation ended. Nobody asked a question, so he left the podium with a polite applause. Then, I stood up to walk down to the first row to change my seat. At the same time, John got up from his chair on the opposite end, carrying some papers and his laptop. He didn't realize at first what was happening, but the audience saw the two of us standing up and became curious. We both walked down the aisle at the same time and speed.

I turned left, he turned right, and we walked toward each other in front of sixty people, investors, and students. I took a deep breath. We would have a presentation together. The audience watched us, looking to the right, to the left, and then to the right again, like a tennis match, wondering what would happen next.

Suddenly and obviously, John seemed to have a shocking realization about why I was there and what could happen to him right then. He stopped his steps in the middle of the arena, stared at me with sheer angst in his eyes, and said out loud:

"Do you want to take the microphone?"

Looking behind him, I could see and hear John's business partners and his girlfriend catching their breaths.

I stopped and looked at him.

"What do you think?"

"If you want to take the microphone, feel free to do so."

He tried to remain calm, but I saw his hands and documents shaking.

"No, go ahead. I just wanted to have a better look at your slides. I will sit right here." I looked at the only free seat in the middle of the first row.

He took a deep breath in relief, walked onto the stage and the speaker's desk, sorted his papers, loaded the presentation slides, turned on the microphone, and started. It took a while till he was ready to start.

"Thank you very much for your time and for allowing me to present our ideas. The team working on the idea is to my right and your left. I am simply representing them as the owner and CEO of the company. All the credits are due to the team. The presentation will go like this: the university has asked me to show only one slide to present the project shortly and then open the room for Q&As to help you better understand what it is all about."

A great start. He played the role of being the eloquent lawyer and creative start-up CEO. While he was talking, he looked at me frequently. I nodded my head to encourage him. I wanted him to win to get my money. After five minutes of introductory words, he opens the Q&A session to the audience.

"Anyone, any questions so far, or is everything clear? I am sure you have a lot of questions!"

He hadn't prepared a presentation, which was disrespectful from my perspective if you want to collect lots of money. Why should someone invest in something they didn't know about? However, he was not allowed to present more than one slide, which was tough.

"Q&A is open. Who wants to start? Please raise your hand," John instructed.

Instantly, I raised my hand without thinking or a plan of why and what to ask.

John looked at me, surprised. At that time, he had no idea who I had become during the last couple of years.

"Yes, what is your question?"

"Hi, thank you for your interesting slide. I am the CEO of a consumer goods company responsible for thousands of people in Central Europe. I want to ask you whether your software program could help to improve the IT performance of the company I am leading."

"Yes, we can."

Encouraged, he explained in detail how it could work.

"Next question?"

He looked around. Another executive raised his hand. John answered professionally. He regained his self-confidence. It dawned on me that he was scared to see me again, not knowing what surprising act I planned for him after the shocking approach to declaring his company bankrupt.

He was very professional and had an in-depth knowledge of the business he was in. Next question. Then, another question. Time passed by very quickly. After an hour, he asked for one last question. I raised my hand for the third time. Again, he answered professionally and enthusiastically. John realized that my questions and my credibility as a CEO helped him convince the investors that it was worth investing in his company.

After the presentation, John walked straight toward me.

"I am so glad that you came. I want to invite you to stay for the reception. I have to talk to some investors, but I will make time for you only afterward."

I nodded my head because I had to talk to him, too. I was on a mission. While he was speaking with some of the investors, I waited alone. The business partners I had known for years didn't come by to say hello. They still remembered what I did to them to get my money back two years prior. I couldn't care less.

Then John came over to me with a glass of wine.

"Thanks a million for your support. I deeply appreciate it. Some investors are very interested. It looks terrific."

"Great news for my ears. You still owe 25,000 euros net, plus the average interest rate for the last two years and the expenses for the court and lawyer. I want my money back. That's why I am here. It looks like you have new investors. So, transferring the money now shouldn't be a problem."

"Well, yes and no. I can't take the money from the company, but I have some private money in a bank account. My aunt died, so I inherited some money from Luxembourg. I will drive there and bring you the money Saturday in a week. Is that okay?"

"You know what? I don't care at all where the money is coming from. I want it back now. If I don't see you and the money next Saturday, I will find you again at one of your keynotes at a conference. And then, I *will* take the microphone and talk about you and your betrayals. That will be the last time you can convince an investor to give you money. You know me. I am serious and not afraid of you. I never was."

I looked at him. When we first met, he saved my life by calling the emergency services. I couldn't believe how we ended up there and didn't understand why.

*　　*　　*

This time, he kept his word. He came to visit me in the apartment he had also lived in. On Saturday, he brought 12,500 euros as his first payment.

"Where is the other half?"

"Please, give me another week, and I will bring the rest next Saturday."

We sat at my dining table and talked about the last two years as if we were good friends who hadn't seen each other for a while. All harmful and painful memories were erased.

The week passed by, and the following Saturday, I expected him to visit and bring the other half. John didn't show up. I called him, left messages on his mobile phone, and sent emails. No response.

I patiently waited for another four weeks. Maybe he had an accident?

After four weeks, I re-dialed his office number from my mobile phone but turned off my ID this time. And there he was, picking up the phone. I realized John hadn't changed at all.

"Hello, this is John. How can I help you?" with his enthusiastic voice, he almost sang into my ears.

I was stunned.

"You are such a jerk. Where is the rest of my money?" I shouted into the phone.

He stumbled.

"I told you, next Saturday . . . it took me a while. I am so sorry."

"Okay. Next Saturday is your final day. If you won't come by and bring the money, you know what will happen soon."

The following Saturday, he finally brought the remaining 12,500 euros. When the doorbell rang, I opened the door, grabbed the envelope, and counted the money while standing in the doorframe. I didn't ask him to come in again.

"Thank you."…I shut the door and left John perplexed. That was it.

*   *   *

Shortly after, I moved back to Munich and resumed my life as a single woman. I was building my business while recovering from all that had happened during the past three years. Over time, my broken heart healed little by little.

A few years later, my friend Sarah and I met at "Schumann's," a famous bar in downtown Munich, for happy hour. Several young men stood behind us, discussing issues about their newly founded start-up company. They were pretty noisy, so I heard more details than I should have. Then I heard his name.

"I met a great lawyer last week. His name is John. He told me he could help us resolve the issue in our favor. He will write a harsh letter to our offenders with his lawyer's address on the letterhead. That will help us to get rid of them. He might join us a little later tonight."

I stopped breathing. I was in shock. I couldn't believe what I was hearing. My heart was beating hard suddenly. Everything inside of me tightened. I was stunned. I turned around and looked at them in astonishment.

Should I tell them who John is and warn them to be careful? He still has no bad feelings about manipulating others and bending the law. He is still convinced he can get away with everything—without paying the price. He is the devil's advocate. I hope he won't show up.

"Why are you shaking your head? What's going on?" Sarah asked.

"Nothing. Nothing. I just had an extraterrestrial experience—an encounter of the third kind. I am sorry. Coincidently, I just had the chance to reconnect with my ex-fiancé or let him go. And in a millisecond, I decided to leave everything behind me, including him. It's finally over. I needed to experience this little 'test.' And I am glad I made the right decision."

I raised my glass.

"Cheers to a wonderful life."

NOTES

1. Gholam Reza Afkhami, *The Life and Times of the Shah* (University of California Press, 2009).

2. Ervand Abrahamian, *A History of Modern Iran* (Cambridge University Press, 2008).

3. Farah Diba-Pahlavi: *Erinnerungen, 2005*

4. Professor A.J. Arberry, *HAFIZ Fifty Poems* (Cambridge University Press, First published 1947; Reprinted 1953, 1962, 1970, 1974)

About the Author

GABRIELE WINTER has worked as an executive coach, trainer, and sparring partner for managers focusing on leadership, career, and resilience for over ten years. She holds a Master of Business Administration degree from the University of Cologne in Germany. She has had a successful career in management, having held positions as a managing director and country manager for US companies in Europe.

Her vast management and leadership skills have supported men and women in stepping up to the next level in their careers, improving their leadership, interpersonal communication skills, and personal resilience.

Gabriele loves to pass on what she has learned and experienced to help others. If you would like to share your story, don't hesitate to reach out to Gabriele by sending an email to info@gabrielewinter.com

9 783982 670201